Math in Focus®
Singapore Math®
by Marshall Cavendish

Transition Guide

For New Program Implementation
and Intervention

Marshall Cavendish
Education

US Distributor

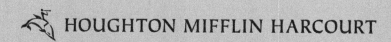

COMMON
CORE

© 2013 Marshall Cavendish International (Singapore) Private Limited

Published by Marshall Cavendish Education
An imprint of Marshall Cavendish International (Singapore) Private Limited
Times Centre, 1 New Industrial Road, Singapore 536196
Customer Service Hotline: (65) 6411 0820
E-mail: tmesales@sg.marshallcavendish.com
Website: www.marshallcavendish.com/education

Common Core Standards © Copyright 2010.
National Governors Association Center for Best Practices and
Council of Chief State School Officers. All rights reserved.

This product is not sponsored or endorsed by the Common Core State Standards
Initiative of the National Governors Association Center for Best Practices and
the Council of Chief State School Officers.

Distributed by
Houghton Mifflin Harcourt
222 Berkeley Street
Boston, MA 02116
Tel: 617-351-5000
Website: www.hmheducation.com/mathinfocus

Cover: © Mike Hill/Getty Images

First published 2013

Math in Focus® Transition Guide Course 3
ISBN 978-0-547-61807-4

Printed in United States of America

6 7 8 1026 17 16 15
4500562833   A B C D E

Math in Focus

Singapore Math
by Marshall Cavendish

Introduction

The *Math in Focus® Transition Guide* provides a map to help transition teachers and students new to the *Math in Focus®* program.

Much of the success of Singapore math is due to the careful way in which algorithms are developed, with an emphasis on understanding. Lessons move from concrete models to pictorial and symbolic representations. Students develop mathematical ideas in depth, and see how the concepts are connected and that mathematics is not a series of isolated skills.

Teaching to Mastery With Student Proficiency

Singapore has been scoring at the top of international comparison studies for over 15 years. One of the key characteristics of the Singapore curriculum is teaching to mastery. This Transition Guide is designed to help teachers as they transition their students into *Math in Focus®*.

What Does Transition Mean?

Transitioning in *Math in Focus®* is the process of using specific methods to teach concepts and skills students have not yet mastered or been exposed to at previous grade levels, so they can attain mastery at their current grade level.

What is the Difference Between Transition and Intervention?

Transition is providing students with the needed exposure to topics and methods that were taught in the previous grade levels. Intervention is serving students who have had repeated exposure and lack mastery. The transition process is beneficial to students who require intervention.

Using the Transition Guide

- *The Transition Guide* Math Background addresses six critical strands: Number Sense (NS), Ratios and Proportional Relationships (RP), Expressions and Equations (EE), Functions (F), Geometry (G), and Statistics and Probability (SP). Additional Math Background support is provided at the beginning of each chapter in the *Math in Focus®* Teacher's Guide.

- The *Math Background* topics were chosen to help teachers understand and apply the Singapore approach upon which *Math in Focus®* is based. These topics are either introduced earlier than in other programs or are presented differently in this program.

- The classroom teacher can easily scan through the *Math Background* to determine the set of skills and concepts taught in prior years. Ensuring that a student has these background skills will help the student succeed in this program.

- For each skill objective, there are *Transition Worksheets*. These worksheets provide step-by-step instruction, practice, and review. A student can follow the steps independently or with someone's help. Corresponding teacher guides provide alternate teaching strategies, checks, and intervention suggestions.

  The *Transition Guide* is also available Online and on the Teacher One-Stop.

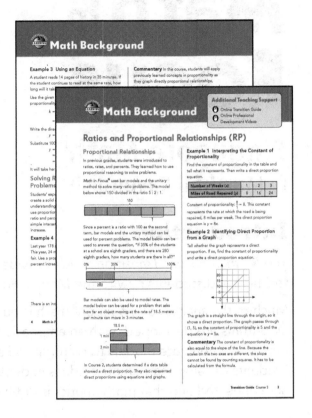

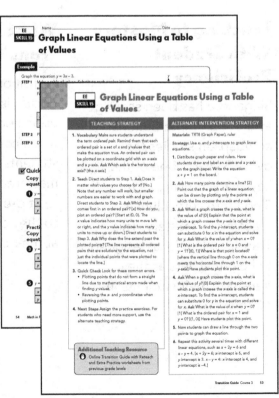

How does a teacher transition students? It's as easy as 1-2-3-4!

1 **Administer diagnostic test.**

Use the items on the Chapter Pre-Test in *Assessments* book to determine whether a student has the necessary prerequisite skills for success in this chapter.

2 **Examine the diagnostic test for each student's strengths and weaknesses.**

Use Recall Prior Knowledge and Quick Check in the *Student Edition* to review concepts and check for understanding.

3 **Determine the instructional pathway for each student.**

Use the Resource Planner in the *Transition Guide* to find the appropriate Math Background and Skills worksheets.

4 **Intervene, reinforce, and assess.**

Use online *Reteach* and *Extra Practice* worksheets from one- or two-grades below.

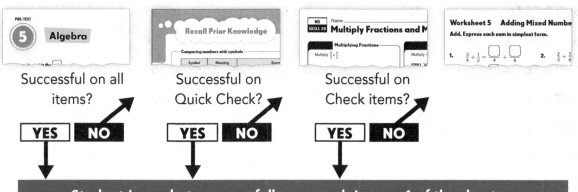

Successful on all items?   YES   NO

Successful on Quick Check?   YES   NO

Successful on Check items?   YES   NO

Student is ready to successfully approach Lesson 1 of the chapter.

Flexible Approach

Depending on your needs, you can also use the Recall Prior Knowledge Quick Check questions in the *Student Edition* to determine whether your students have the prerequisite skills for a chapter. The Chapter Pre-Test in the *Assessments* book can then serve as a check for understanding. You can also bypass Step 1 or Step 2.

Course 3 Contents

Course 3 Resource Planner

TRANSITION SKILLS AND RESOURCES

STRAND/ SKILL	SKILL OBJECTIVE	ASSESSMENTS PRE-TEST	STUDENT BOOK
NS 1	Interpret the real number system.	Chapter 1: Items 1–2	Ch1 RPK, QC 1
NS 2	Write terminating or repeating decimals.	Chapter 1: Items 3–6	Ch1 RPK, QC 2–5
NS 3	Locate irrational numbers on a number line.	Chapter 1: Items 7–8	Ch1 RPK, QC 6–7
NS 4	Add integers.	Chapter 1: Item 9	Ch1 RPK, QC 8
NS 5	Subtract integers.	Chapter 1: Item 10	Ch1 RPK, QC 9
NS 6	Multiply integers.	Chapter 1: Item 11	Ch1 RPK, QC 10
NS 7	Divide integers.	Chapter 1: Item 12	Ch1 RPK, QC 11
NS 8	Multiply decimals by positive powers of 10.	Chapter 2: Items 1–4	Ch2 RPK, QC 1–3
NS 9	Divide decimals by positive powers of 10.	Chapter 2: Items 6–9	Ch2 RPK, QC 4–6
EE 10	Identify equivalent equations.	Chapter 3: Items 1–4	Ch3 RPK, QC 1–4
EE 11	Write a linear equation to relate two quantities.	Chapter 3: Items 5–8	Ch3 RPK, QC 5–8
EE 12	Solve algebraic equations.	Chapter 3: Items 9–12	Ch3 RPK, QC 9–12
NS 13	Represent fractions as repeating decimals.	Chapter 3: Items 13–16	Ch3 RPK, QC 13–16
RP 14	Recognize direct proportion in graphs.	Chapter 4: Items 1–8	Ch4 RPK, QC 1–2
EE 15	Graph linear equations using a table of values.	Chapter 5: Items 1–2	Ch5 RPK, QC 1–2
EE 16	Solve real-world problems algebraically.	Chapter 5: Items 3–4	Ch5 RPK, QC 3
EE 17	Writing algebraic expressions to represent unknown quantities.	Chapter 6 Items 1–2	Ch6 RPK, QC 1–2
EE 18	Evaluate algebraic expressions.	Chapter 6: Items 3–4	Ch6 RPK, QC 3–6
EE 19	Understand squares and square roots.	Chapter 7: Items 1–4	Ch7 RPK, QC 1–6
EE 20	Understand cubes and cube roots.	Chapter 7: Items 5–8	Ch7 RPK, QC 7–12
G 21	Find lengths of horizontal and vertical line segments in the coordinate plane.	Chapter 7: Items 9–10	Ch7 RPK, QC 13–16
G 22	Find the volume of prisms and pyramids.	Chapter 7: Item 14	Ch7 RPK, QC 20–21

KEY: RPK (Recall Prior Knowledge), QC (Quick Check), C (Course)

ONLINE RESOURCES ONLY

C2 RETEACH	C2 EXTRA PRACTICE	C1 RETEACH	C1 EXTRA PRACTICE
C2A pp. 18–19	C2A Lesson 1.4		
C2A pp. 8–14	C2A Lesson 1.2		
C2A pp. 15–17	C2A Lesson 1.3		
C2A pp. 25–33	C2A Lesson 2.1		
C2A pp. 34–38	C2A Lesson 2.2		
C2A pp. 39–40	C2A Lesson 2.3		
C2A pp. 41–44	C2A Lessons 2.3, 2.4		
C2A pp. 54–60	C2A Lesson 2.6	C1A pp. 55–61	C1A Lesson 3.2
C2A pp. 54–60	C2A Lesson 2.6	C1A pp. 62–68	C1A Lesson 3.3
C2A pp. 89–91	C2A Lesson 4.1	C1B pp. 1–15	C1B Lesson 8.1
C2A pp. 126–144	C2A Lesson 5.2	C1B pp. 16–32	C1B Lesson 8.2
C2A pp. 92–101	C2A Lesson 4.2	C1B pp. 1–15	C1B Lesson 8.1
C2A pp. 8–14	C2A Lesson 1.2		
C2A pp. 119–144	C2A Lessons 5.1–5.3		
C2A pp. 126–144	C2A Lessons 5.2, 5.3	C1B pp. 70–73	C1B Lesson 9.3
C2A pp. 102–106	C2A Lesson 4.3	C1B pp. 33–39	C1B Lesson 8.4
C2A pp. 81–88	C2A Lessons 3.6, 3.7	C1A pp.171–184, 198–206	C1A Lessons 7.1, 7.5
C2A pp. 61–72	C2A Lessons 3.1–3.3	C1A pp. 185–186	C1A Lesson 7.2
		C1A pp. 28–29	C1A Lesson 1.4
		C1A pp. 30–32	C1A Lesson 1.5
		C1B pp. 48–63	C1B Lesson 9.2
C2B pp.68–75	C2B Lesson 8.3	C1B pp. 133–156	C1B Lessons 12.2, 12.3, 12.4

Course 3 Resource Planner

TRANSITION SKILLS AND RESOURCES

STRAND/ SKILL	SKILL OBJECTIVE	ASSESSMENTS PRE-TEST	STUDENT BOOK
G 23	Find the volume of cones, cylinders, and spheres.	Chapter 7: Items 11–13	Ch7 RPK, QC 17–19
G 24	Recognize a symmetric point on the coordinate plane.	Chapter 8: Items 1–3	Ch8 RPK, QC 1–4
RP 25	Identify directly proportional quantities.	Chapter 8: Items 4–7	Ch8 RPK, QC 5–7
G 26	Recognize perpendicular bisectors.	Chapter 8: Items 8–9	Ch8 RPK, QC 8–10
RP 27	Identify the scale factor in diagrams.	Chapter 9: Items 1–2	Ch9 RPK, QC 1–3
RP 28	Solve problems involving scale drawings or models.	Chapter 9: Items 3–4	Ch9 RPK, QC 4–6
G 29	Find measures of interior angles of a triangle.	Chapter 9: Item 5	Ch9 RPK, QC 7–9
G 30	Find measures of exterior angles of a triangle.	Chapter 9: Item 6	Ch9 RPK, QC 10–11
G 31	Find measures of angles formed by parallel lines and a transversal.	Chapter 9: Items 7–8	Ch9 RPK, QC 12-13
SP 32	Finding relative frequencies.	Chapter 10 Items 1–2	Ch10 RPK, QC 1
SP 33	Find the probability of a simple event.	Chapter 11 Items 1–5	Ch11 RPK, QC 1–5
SP 34	Identify mutually exclusive events.	Chapter 11 Items 6–9	Ch11 RPK, QC 6–9

🖱 ONLINE RESOURCES ONLY

C2 RETEACH	C2 EXTRA PRACTICE	C1 RETEACH	C1 EXTRA PRACTICE
C2B pp. 64–79	C2B Lessons 8.2–8.4		
		C1B pp. 40–47	C1B Lesson 9.1
C2A pp. 119–131	C2A Lessons 5.1, 5.2		
C2B pp. 35–37	C2B Lesson 7.2		
C2B pp. 51–60	C2B Lesson 7.5		
C2B pp. 51–60	C2B Lesson 7.5		
C2B pp. 23–29	C2B Lesson 6.4		
C2B pp. 23–29	C2B Lesson 6.4		
C2B pp. 20–22	C2B Lesson 6.3		
C2B pp. 131–139	C2B Lesson 10.3	C1B pp.157–163	C1B Lesson 13.1
C2B pp. 117–130	C2B Lesson 10.2		
C2B pp. 117–130	C2B Lesson 10.2		

Math Background

The Number System (NS)

The Real Numbers

Students have learned that whole numbers, fractions, decimals, and integers are part of a larger set called the *real number system*. The set of real numbers consists of two subsets—rational numbers and irrational numbers.

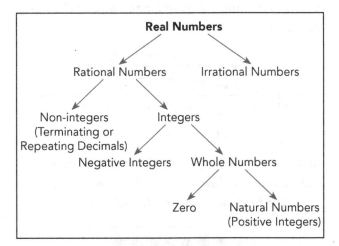

Students learned to identify real-number properties and apply them to mathematical and real-world problems. One property of the real numbers is the following: For any two real numbers a and b: $a = b$, $a > b$, or $a < b$. Students applied this property when they learned to order real numbers.

Example 1 Order Real Numbers

Order this list of real numbers from least to greatest using the symbol <.

$$-\frac{15}{8}, \frac{\pi}{2}, -\sqrt{17}, \frac{13}{9}, -2\frac{3}{16}$$

Represent each real number in decimal form to 4 decimal places.

$$-\frac{15}{8} = -1.8750 \qquad \frac{\pi}{2} \approx 1.5708 \qquad -\sqrt{17} \approx -4.1231$$

$$\frac{13}{9} \approx 1.4444 \qquad -2\frac{3}{16} = -2.1875$$

Write the original numbers in order.

$$-\sqrt{17} < -2\frac{3}{16} < -\frac{15}{8} < \frac{13}{9} < \frac{\pi}{2}$$

Commentary One way to compare the size of irrational numbers is to locate them approximately on a number line. To do this, students used the fact that every number has a decimal expansion, learning that the decimal expansions for irrational numbers are non-repeating and non-terminating.

Example 2 Graph Irrational Numbers

Graph $\sqrt{55}$ on the number line using rational approximations.

Find an approximate value for $\sqrt{55}$ by using a calculator.

$$\sqrt{55} = 7.4161985$$

$\sqrt{55}$ lies between 7.4 and 7.5. It is quite close to 7.4.

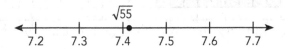

Commentary Students have learned to recognize different forms of rational numbers—fractions, decimals, percents—and they can show that the decimal expansion of a rational number repeats eventually.

Example 3 Write Rational Numbers as Repeating Decimals

Write the rational number $\frac{11}{6}$ as a repeating decimal. Divide the numerator by the denominator. Keep dividing until the digits in the quotient show a repeating pattern.

$$\begin{array}{r} 1.833 \\ 6\overline{)11.000} \end{array}$$

$$\frac{11}{6} = 1.8\overline{3}$$

Number Representations

Students have used many visual models for numbers. For example, they used a number line like the one below to illustrate how to interpret absolute value as magnitude for a positive or negative quantity.

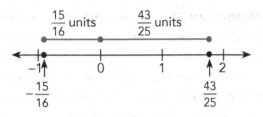

Ten-by-ten grids were used to introduce students to decimal and percent concepts. A model like the one below could be used to connect a grid representation to the real number line.

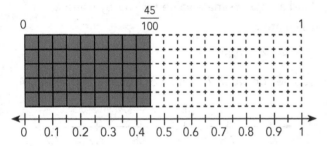

Multiple number lines helped students compare rational numbers in fraction and decimal forms.

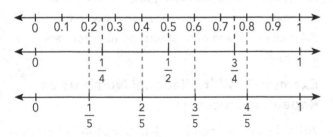

In the diagram below, $\frac{32}{9}$ and $\frac{29}{8}$ are compared by first changing the numbers to decimal form.

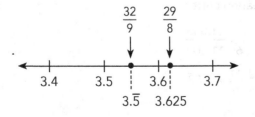

Students also used both number-line models and counters to understand integer operations. In this example, students saw that $p + q$ is a number located a distance $|q|$ from p.

Example 4 Adding Integers

Evaluate $-8 + 3$.

To add on a number line, start at 0 and move 8 units in the negative direction. Then, from -8, move 3 units in the positive direction to arrive at -5. The sum is -5.

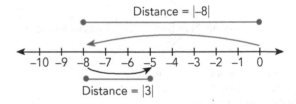

To add with counters, show -8 with 8 red counters and $+3$ with 3 yellow counters. Remove three zero pairs. The final model shows the sum, -5.

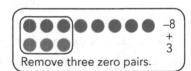

Remove three zero pairs.

Students using *Math in Focus*® have not only learned fundamental number concepts, but have had numerous opportunities to solve problems involving operations with rational numbers. In later courses, they will learn about numbers that are not real, such as imaginary numbers and complex numbers.

Additional Teaching Resource

For additional reading, see *The Singapore Model Method for Learning Mathematics* published by the Ministry of Education of Singapore and *Bar Modeling: A Problem-Solving Tool* by Yeap Ban Har, published by Marshall Cavendish Education.

Math Background

Ratios and Proportional Relationships (RP)

Proportional Relationships

In previous grades, students were introduced to ratios. They learned how to use proportional reasoning to solve problems.

Math in Focus® uses bar models and the unitary method to solve many ratio problems. The model below shows 150 divided in the ratio 5 : 2 : 1.

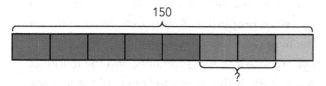

Since a percent is a ratio with 100 as the second term, bar models and the unitary method can be used for percent problems. The model below can be used to answer the question, "If 35% of the students at a school are eighth graders, and there are 280 eighth graders, how many students are there in all?"

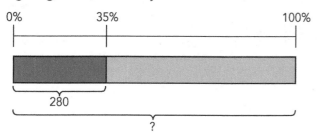

Bar models can also be used to model rates. The model below be used for a problem that asks how far an object moving at the rate of 18.5 meters per minute can move in 3 minutes.

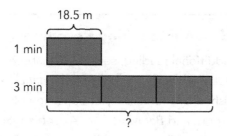

In Course 2, students determined if a data table showed a direct proportion. They also repesented direct proportions using equations and graphs.

Example 1 Interpreting the Constant of Proportionality

Find the constant of proportionality in the table and tell what it represents. Then write a direct proportion equation.

Number of Weeks (x)	1	2	3
Miles of Road Repaired (y)	8	16	24

Constant of proportionality: $\frac{8}{1} = 8$. This constant represents the rate at which the road is being repaired, 8 miles per week. The direct proportion equation is $y = 8x$.

Example 2 Identifying Direct Proportion from a Graph

Tell whether the graph represents a direct proportion. If so, find the constant of proportionality and write a direct proportion equation.

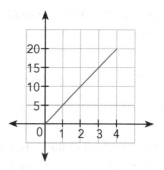

The graph is a straight line through the origin, so it shows a direct proportion. The graph passes through (1, 5), so the constant of proportionality is 5 and the equation is $y = 5x$.

Example 3 Using an Equation

A student reads 14 pages of history in 35 minutes. If the student continues to read at the same rate, how long will it take her to read 100 more pages?

Use the given information to find a constant of proportionality.

$$k = \frac{35 \text{ minutes}}{14 \text{ pages}}$$
$$= 2.5 \text{ minutes per page}$$

Write the direct proportion equation.
$$y = 2.5x$$

Substitute 100 for x and solve for y.
$$y = 2.5x$$
$$= 2.5 \cdot 100$$
$$= 250$$

It will take her 250 minutes to read 100 more pages.

Solving Ratio and Percent Problems

Students' experiences with data tables and graphs create a solid conceptual foundation for understanding direct proportion. Then, students can use proportional relationships to solve multistep ratio and percent problems: for example, problems about simple interest, tax, commissions, and percent increase.

Example 4 Direct Proportion and Percent

Last year 178 students competed in the science fair. This year, 24 more students have signed up for the fair. Use a proportion to find the approximate percent increase in the number of students.

$$x\% : 100\% = 24 : 178$$
$$\frac{x}{100} = \frac{24}{178}$$
$$100 \cdot \frac{x}{100} = 100 \cdot \frac{24}{178}$$
$$x = 13.5$$

There is an increase of about 13.5%.

Commentary In this course, students will apply previously learned concepts in proportionality as they graph directly proportional relationships, interpreting the unit rate as the slope of the graph. And, they will use similar triangles to explain why the slope m is the same between any two distinct points on a non-vertical line.

Ratio and proportion continue to be important topics in later math courses. For example, in high school geometry students will learn that a line parallel to one side of a triangle divides the other two sides proportionally. Also, the altitude drawn to the hypotenuse of a right triangle divides the hypotenuse into two segments, and the length of the altitude is the geometric mean of the lengths of these segments.

Additional Teaching Resource

For additional reading, see *The Singapore Model Method for Learning Mathematics* published by the Ministry of Education of Singapore and *Bar Modeling: A Problem-Solving Tool* by Yeap Ban Har, published by Marshall Cavendish Education.

Additional Teaching Support

 Online Transition Guide

Online Professional Development Videos

Expressions and Equations (EE)

From Concrete to Abstract

Earlier levels of *Math in Focus®* provided a strong foundation in using bar models to model and solve equations. As a result, students in Course 3 are ready to view an equation as more than a collection of numbers and letters. Rather, an equation describes a relationship between numbers, proportional quantities, or bivariate quantities involving two variables.

The equations themselves are growing more complex. In Course 3, students encounter equations containing exponents and radicals, equations that require application of the distributive property and other algebraic properties before they can be solved, equations that students solve for a variable, equations involving negative integers, equations with no solution, and equations with an infinite number of solutions. Using a bar model to solve an equation containing, say, an exponent and a coefficient, while not impossible, is less practicable than solving it using conventional algebraic methods, particularly if one understands the logic behind those methods. The development of the mathematics in these chapters is designed to help students do just that.

Students learn that just as multiplication is repeated addition, exponentiation is repeated multiplication when the exponents are a positive whole number. They simplify exponential expressions using the various properties of exponents. Exploring the rationale behind these properties enables them to make subtle distinctions.

$$2^3 \cdot 2^5 = 2^{3+5} = 2^8$$
$$\text{BUT}$$
$$(2^3)^5 = 2^{3 \cdot 5} = 2^{15}$$

The study of exponents, a shorthand way of writing multiplication, leads naturally to scientific notation, a shorthand way of writing very large and very small numbers.

$$93{,}000{,}000 = 9.3 \cdot 10^7$$
$$0.0000372 = 3.72 \cdot 10^{-5}$$

Students solve a variety of equations in one variable. They begin by applying properties of equality to solve algebraic equations and to solve real-world problems. Their work with one-variable equations is then connected to two-variable linear equations and using slope-intercept form: $y = mx + b$.

Students get the opportunity to explore many of the intriguing aspects of the equation $y = mx + b$. By associating x and y with the coordinates of the point (x, y) in the coordinate plane, this equation can be graphed. In previous courses students have learned to plot points to graph lines. Now they will do so by using the slope m and the y-intercept b. They will see that proportions represent a special type of linear equation, one in which m is the constant of proportionality and b equals 0.

Most important for their future study of mathematics, they will observe the fundamental relationship between a graph and its equation: The coordinates of every point on the graph satisfy the equation, and every ordered pair (x, y) that satisfies the equation is a point on the graph. This provides a method they will use to solve a system of two equations. The solution is the point (x, y) where the graphs intersect.

Understanding Exponents

Simplifying exponential expressions involves understanding and applying basic properties.

Example 1 Using Properties of Exponents

Rewrite the expression with a single exponent.

$$\frac{3^2 \cdot 3^7 \cdot 4^9}{(12^3)^2}$$

Simplifying this expression requires the use of several properties.

$$\frac{3^2 \cdot 3^7 \cdot 4^9}{(12^3)^2} = \frac{3^9 \cdot 4^9}{(12^3)^2} \quad \text{Product of Powers Property}$$

$$= \frac{12^9}{(12^3)^2} \quad \text{Power of a Product Property}$$

$$= \frac{12^9}{12^6} \quad \text{Power of a Power Property}$$

$$= 12^3 \quad \text{Quotient of Powers Property}$$

Commentary By the Power of a Product Property, when a product is raised to a power, all factors in the product must be raised to the given power. So, $(3 \cdot 4)^9 = 3^9 \cdot 4^9$. Step 2 of Example 1 shows how this property can be used in the reverse direction: $3^9 \cdot 4^9 = (3 \cdot 4)^9 = 12^9$. The Power of a Quotient Property can be used in reverse, too: $\frac{6^5}{2^5} = \left(\frac{6}{2}\right)^5 = 3^5$.

Example 2 Writing Prime Factorizations Using Exponential Notation

Write the prime factorization of 540.

First, use divisibility rules to write the prime factors.
$$540 = 2 \cdot 2 \cdot 3 \cdot 3 \cdot 3 \cdot 5$$

Now write the prime factorization using exponents.
$$540 = 2^2 \cdot 3^3 \cdot 5$$

In Course 3, students learn to interpret integer exponents, including 0 and negative exponents.

Example 3 Interpreting an Exponent of Zero

Simplify $\frac{4^5 \cdot 4^3}{4^8}$.

$$\frac{4^5 \cdot 4^3}{4^8} = \frac{4^8}{4^8} \quad \text{Product of Powers Property}$$

$$= 4^0 \quad \text{Quotient of Powers Property}$$

$$= 1 \quad \text{Simplify.}$$

Commentary Students may be uncomfortable with the idea that any non-zero number raised to the zero power equals 1. Ths definition is necessary so that the Product of Powers and Quotient of Powers Properties are valid for exponents other than positive whole numbers.

Example 4 Interpreting Negative Exponents

Rewrite 5^{-3} using a positive exponent.

For any nonzero real number a, and any integer n, $a^{-n} = \frac{1}{a^n}$.

$$5^{-3} = \frac{1}{5^3} = \frac{1}{125}$$

Example 5 Using Squares and Cubes

Evaluate $\sqrt{64} + \sqrt[3]{64}$.

$$\sqrt{64} + \sqrt[3]{64} = 8 + \sqrt[3]{64} \quad \text{Because } 64 = 8 \cdot 8$$

$$= 8 + 4 \quad \text{Because } 64 = 4 \cdot 4 \cdot 4$$

$$= 12$$

Commentary The square root symbol $\sqrt{\ }$ indicates the positive square root. So, $\sqrt{64} = 8$. Use a negative sign with the radical symbol to indicate the negative square root: $-\sqrt{64} = -8$.

Scientific Notation

Scientific notation is an application of exponents that is practical as well as motivational. It provides a way to write very large and very small numbers compactly. And because those numbers describe fascinating quantities such as weights of atoms and diameters of galaxies, scientific notation carries a built-in incentive for students to master the material.

Example 6 Writing Numbers in Scientific Notation

Write 6,400,000 and 0.00091 in scientific notation.

A number written in scientific notation consists of a coefficient greater than or equal to 1 and less than 10, and a power of 10. To find the coefficient of 6,400,000, move the decimal point at the end of the number 6 places to the left. This is equivalent to dividing by 1,000,000. So as not to change the number, multiply it by 1,000,000 as well. ($1,000,000 = 10^6$)

$$6,400,000 = 6.4 \cdot 10^6$$

To find the coefficient of 0.00091, move the decimal point 4 places to the right. This is equivalent to multiplying by 10,000. So as not to change the number, divide it by 10,000 as well. $\left(\dfrac{1}{10,000} = 10^{-4}\right)$

$$0.00091 = 9.1 \cdot 10^{-4}$$

Commentary Converting numbers from standard to scientific notation and vice-versa can become a mechanical process of counting decimal places, writing the coefficient, and then using the number of places moved as the exponent on 10. After students identify a coefficient, encourage students to think: 6.4 times what power of 10 will equal 6,400,000? The power, 1,000,000, can be written as 10^6.

Example 7 Adding and Subtracting With the Same and Different Powers of 10

a) Find the sum: $7.93 \cdot 10^5 + 9.02 \cdot 10^5$.

$$
\begin{aligned}
7.93 \cdot 10^5 + 9.02 \cdot 10^5 &= (7.93 + 9.02) \cdot 10^5 \\
&= 16.95 \cdot 10^5 \\
&= 1.695 \cdot 10^1 \cdot 10^5 \\
&= 1.695 \cdot 10^{1+5} \\
&= 1.695 \cdot 10^6
\end{aligned}
$$

b) Find the difference: $3.8 \cdot 10^{-4} - 7.1 \cdot 10^{-5}$.

$$
\begin{aligned}
3.8 \cdot 10^{-4} - 7.1 \cdot 10^{-5} &= 3.8 \cdot 10^{-4} - 0.71 \cdot 10^{-4} \\
&= (3.8 - 0.71) \cdot 10^{-4} \\
&= 3.09 \cdot 10^{-4}
\end{aligned}
$$

Example 8 Adding and Subtracting Numbers with Different Units

Find the sum: $550,000,000 \text{ m} + 3.18 \cdot 10^6 \text{ km}$.

First, rewrite one of the quantities in the same unit as the other quantity and in scientific notation.

$$
\begin{aligned}
550,000,000 \text{ m} &= 550,000 \text{ km} \\
&= 5.5 \cdot 10^5 \text{ km}
\end{aligned}
$$

Now add.

$$
\begin{aligned}
5.5 \cdot 10^5 + 3.18 \cdot 10^6 &= 5.5 \cdot 10^5 + 31.8 \cdot 10^5 \\
&= (5.5 + 31.8) \cdot 10^5 \\
&= 37.3 \cdot 10^5 \\
&= 3.73 \cdot 10^1 \cdot 10^5 \\
&= 3.73 \cdot 10^{1+5} \\
&= 3.73 \cdot 10^6
\end{aligned}
$$

When writing real-world measurements in either standard form or scientific notation, students should choose units that are appropriate to the situation and manageable. The height of a doorway may be 0.00133 miles, but 7 feet is a far more useful way to express the height. This caveat is particularly true when writing very large or very small quantities.

To multiply and divide numbers in scientific notation, students apply the Product of Powers Property and the Quotient of Powers Property. They learn that these products and quotients should also be written in scientific notation.

Example 9 Multiplying and Dividing in Scientific Notation

a) Find the product: $(3.5 \cdot 10^4)(4.6 \cdot 10^{-7})$.

$$(3.5 \cdot 10^4)(4.6 \cdot 10^{-7}) = (3.5 \cdot 4.6)(10^4 \cdot 10^{-7})$$
$$= 16.1 \cdot 10^{4+(-7)}$$
$$= 16.1 \cdot 10^{-3}$$
$$= 1.61 \cdot 10^{-2}$$

b) Find the quotient: $(8.46 \cdot 10^{13}) \div (4.7 \cdot 10^5)$.

$$(8.46 \cdot 10^{13})(4.7 \cdot 10^5) = \frac{8.46 \cdot 10^{13}}{4.7 \cdot 10^5}$$
$$= \frac{8.46}{4.7} \cdot \frac{10^{13}}{10^5}$$
$$= 1.8 \cdot 10^{13-5}$$
$$= 1.8 \cdot 10^8$$

Linear Equations

Chapters 3 and 4 focus on solving one-step linear equations, writing two-variable linear equations, and graphing them.

When solving equations with fractions, students can use the technique of multiplying both sides by the least common multiple of all the denominators.

Example 10 Solving Linear Equations

Solve for x: $\dfrac{3(4x-5)}{5} + \dfrac{x+4}{3} = 12$.

$$\frac{3(4x-5)}{5} + \frac{x+4}{3} = 12$$
$$15\left(\frac{3(4x-5)}{5} + \frac{x+4}{3}\right) = 15 \cdot 12$$
$$3[3(4x-5)] + 5(x+4) = 180$$
$$9(4x-5) + 5x + 20 = 180$$
$$36x - 45 + 5x + 20 = 180$$
$$41x = 205$$
$$x = 5$$

Solving linear equations serves as a method for writing a repeating decimal as a fraction.

Example 11 Writing Repeating Decimals as Fractions

Write $0.\overline{7}$ as a fraction.

Let $x = 0.\overline{7}$.

$$\begin{aligned} \text{Then } 10x &= 7.7777\ldots \\ -\,x &= 0.7777\ldots \\ 9x &= 7 \\ x &= \frac{7}{9} \end{aligned}$$

Every linear equation of the form $ax + b = 0$, with $a \neq 0$, has exactly one solution. A first-degree equation (an equation in x to the first power) may have no solutions (an *inconsistent* equation) or an infinite number of solutions (an *identity*). An equation is inconsistent if the solution leads to a false statement, such as $3 = 1$. An equation is an identity if the solution leads to a statement that is always true, such as $2 = 2$.

Example 12 Inconsistent Equations

Solve: $2(x + 2) - x = x + 7$.

$$2(x + 2) - x = x + 7$$
$$2(x + 2) = x + x + 7$$
$$2x + 4 = 2x + 7$$
$$4 = 7$$

Since $4 \neq 7$, the equation is inconsistent. It has no solution.

Example 13 Identities

Solve: $3(3x - 2) + 2x = 11x - 6$.

$$3(3x - 2) + 2x = 11x - 6$$
$$9x - 6 + 2x = 11x - 6$$
$$11x - 6 = 11x - 6$$
$$-6 = -6$$

Since $-6 = -6$, the equation is an identity. It has an infinite number of solutions.

In Chapter 3, students express relationships between two variables using tables of values and equations, evaluate equations for given values of the variables, and solve for one of the two variables.

Example 14 Expressing Relationships Between Two Variables

Bicycle rentals cost $6 per hour. Let x represent the number of hours a bike is rented, and let y represent the total cost. Express the relationship between x and y using a table of values and an equation.

x (time in hours)	1	2	3	4	5
y (cost in dollars)	6	12	18	24	30

To find the cost, multiply the number of hours, x, by the cost per hour, 6. So, $y = 6x$.

Commentary In Chapter 4, students connect what they know about two-variable linear equations with graphs. The graph of $y = 6x$ is a line through the origin, whose slope, 6, is a unit rate of change, $6 per 1 hour. The equation $y = 6x + 10$ could represent the total cost of renting a bike at $6 per hour, plus a $10 fee. Its graph is also a line with slope 6, but one that passes through the point (0, 10).

Also in preparation for graphing and solving problems, students learn to solve a two-variable equation for one of the variables.

Example 15 Solving a Linear Equation for a Variable

Express y in terms of x: $3(x - 3y) = -15x + 7$.

$$3(x - 3y) = -15x + 7$$
$$3x - 9y = -15x + 7$$
$$-9y = -15x - 3x + 7$$
$$-9y = -18 + 7$$
$$\frac{-9y}{-9} = \frac{-18x}{-9} + \frac{7}{-9}$$
$$y = 2x - \frac{7}{9}$$

Lines and Linear Equations

In Chapter 4, students apply much of what they have learned in earlier chapters to analyzing lines drawn on the coordinate plane, and to graphing linear equations. Building on their intuitive notions of slope and intercept, students use various clues about lines to graph the lines and write their equations. They also revisit the subject of proportionality, which they have studied in earlier courses, and see that a proportional relationship between two quantities is a special case of a linear relationship, one that graphs as a line whose slope is the constant of proportionality.

Example 16 Finding Slopes of Lines

Using Rise and Run

Between two points on a line, the rise is −6 and the run is 8. Find the slope of the line.

$$\text{slope} = \frac{\text{rise}}{\text{run}}$$
$$= \frac{-6}{8}$$
$$= -\frac{3}{4}$$

Using Two Points on the Line

Find the slope of the line that passes through the points $(6, -7)$ and $(-4, 13)$.

$$\text{slope} = \frac{y_2 - y_1}{x_2 - x_1}$$
$$= \frac{13 - (-7)}{-4 - 6}$$
$$= \frac{20}{-10}$$
$$= -2$$

Commentary When two points are used to find a slope, it makes no difference which is designated (x_1, y_1) and which (x_2, y_2). The better choice is usually the one that promises easier calculations.

Students can use visual clues to make predictions about lines. A line that slants upward to the right has positive slope. A line that slants downward to the right has negative slope. Parallel lines have equal slope. Horizontal lines have slope of zero. Vertical lines have undefined slope.

Example 17 Finding Slopes in Real-World Situations

A redwood tree grew at a steady annual rate. A graph of the tree's height, y, in feet, after x years, passes through the points $(16, 104)$ and $(22, 143)$. What is the slope of the line, and what does it represent?

$$\text{slope} = \frac{y_2 - y_1}{x_2 - x_1}$$
$$= \frac{143 - 104}{22 - 16}$$
$$= \frac{39}{6}$$
$$= 6.5$$

The slope is 6.5. It represents the tree's rate of growth in feet per year. (The tree grew 6.5 feet per year.)

Example 18 Finding Slopes and Intercepts of Graphs of Linear Equations

Find the slope and y-intercept of the graph of the equation $2x - 3y = 15$.

Rewrite the equation in $y = mx + b$ form.

$$2x - 3y = 15$$
$$-3y = -2x + 15$$
$$\frac{-3y}{-3} = \frac{-2x}{-3} + \frac{15}{-3}$$
$$y = \frac{2}{3}x - 5$$

The slope is $\frac{2}{3}$. The y-intercept is −5.

Example 19 Finding an Equation of a Line

Write an equation of the line that passes through the pair of points (–1, 9) and (3, 1).

Find the slope of the line.

$$\text{slope} = \frac{y_2 - y_1}{x_2 - x_1}$$

$$= \frac{1 - 9}{3 - (-1)}$$

$$= \frac{-8}{4}$$

$$= -2$$

Now use the slope and the point (3, 1) to find the y-intercept.

$$y = mx + b$$

$$1 = -2(3) + b$$

$$7 = b$$

So, an equation of the line is $y = -2x + 7$.

Example 20 Drawing a Graph of a Line

Graph a line with slope $-\frac{2}{3}$ that passes through the point (2, 4).

Plot (2, 4). Then use the given slope to plot a second point, at (5, 2). Draw a line through the two points.

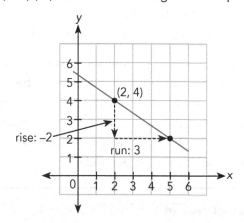

Systems of Equations

A set of linear equations in two variables is called a *system of linear equations*. Students learn that a system of two linear equations can have one solution, infinitely many solutions, or no solutions.

Example 21 Solving a System of Linear Equations by the Elimination Method

Solve the following system of equations.

$$2x + 3y = 2 \qquad \text{Equation 1}$$
$$3x - 4y = -14 \qquad \text{Equation 2}$$

Multiply Equation 1 by 4 and call it Equation 3.

$$4(2x + 3y) = 4 \cdot 2$$
$$8x + 12y = 8 \qquad \text{Equation 3}$$

Multiply Equation 2 by 3 and call it Equation 4.

$$3(3x - 4y) = 3(-14)$$
$$9x - 12y = -42 \qquad \text{Equation 4}$$

Add Equation 3 and Equation 4 and solve for x.

$$8x + 12y = 8$$
$$\underline{9x - 12y = -42}$$
$$17x = -34$$
$$x = -2$$

Find y by substituting $x = -2$ into either equation.

$$2x + 3y = 2 \qquad \text{Equation 1}$$
$$2(-2) + 3y = 2$$
$$3y = 6$$
$$y = 2$$

So, the solution of the system is (–2, 2).

Commentary Students should understand that there are an infinite number of (x, y) values that make either one of the original equations in the system above true. But the solution (–2, 2) represents the only x- and y-values that make both of the original equations true statements.

Example 22 Solving a System of Linear Equations by the Substitution Method

Solve the following system of equations.

$$3x - 2y = -3 \qquad \text{Equation 1}$$
$$3x + y = 3 \qquad \text{Equation 2}$$

Solve Equation 2 for y.

$$3x + y = 3$$
$$y = 3 - 3x$$

Now substitute this expression for y into Equation 1 and solve for x.

$$3x - 2y = -3$$
$$3x - 2(3 - 3x) = -3$$
$$3x - 6 + 6x = -3$$
$$9x - 6 = -3$$
$$9x = 3$$
$$x = \frac{1}{3}$$

Find y by substituting $x = \frac{1}{3}$ into either equation.

$$3x + y = 3 \qquad \text{Equation 2}$$
$$3\left(\frac{1}{3}\right) + y = 3$$
$$1 + y = 3$$
$$y = 2$$

So, the solution of the system is $\left(\frac{1}{3}, 2\right)$.

Students learn that the graphs of a system of linear equations present three possible cases: (1) The graphs of the equations intersect at a point whose coordinates are the solution of the system; (2) the graphs are parallel, so there is no point whose coordinates are a solution; or (3) the graphs are the same line, in which case the coordinates of every point are solutions.

A system of equations with no solutions is called an *inconsistent system*. A system with an infinite number of solutions is called a *dependent system*.

Example 23 Identifying an Inconsistent System of Equations

State whether the system of equations is inconsistent.

$$6x + y = 3 \qquad \text{Equation 1}$$
$$\frac{1}{2}y = -3x - 1 \qquad \text{Equation 2}$$

Rewrite both equations in slope-intercept form. Then compare the equations.

$$y = -6x + 3 \qquad \text{Equation 1}$$
$$y = -6x - 2 \qquad \text{Equation 2}$$

The graphs of the equations have the same slope but different y-intercepts. So the lines are parallel, and and there are no ordered pairs that make both equations true. So, the system has no solution and is inconsistent.

Example 24 Identifying a Dependent System of Equations

State whether the system of equations is dependent.

$$-3x + 5y = 12 \qquad \text{Equation 1}$$
$$-12x + 20y = 48 \qquad \text{Equation 2}$$

Notice that Equation 2 is 4 times Equation 1. This means that the equations are equivalent. The graphs of the equations are concurrent. So, there are an infinite number of ordered pairs that make both equations true. Because the system has an infinite number of solutions, it is dependent.

Additional Teaching Resource

For additional reading, see *The Singapore Model Method for Learning Mathematics* published by the Ministry of Education of Singapore and *Bar Modeling*: *A Problem-Solving Tool* by Yeap Ban Har, published by Marshall Cavendish Education.

Math Background

Additional Teaching Support

 Online Transition Guide

Online Professional Development Videos

Functions (F)

Formalizing a Familiar Idea

Chapter 6 explores the concept of a function, a rule that states how to transform one quantity into another. The rule "Add 5 to the number that I name," is a function. The rule transforms the number 7 into 12 and the number 9 into 14. Additionally, the rule illustrates the primary requirement of a function: It assures that there is one and only one quantity into which a given quantity can be transformed.

Other examples of functions include areas (the area of a rectangle is a unique quantity found by multiplying the length times the width) and prime factorizations (there is one and only one prime factorization of a given positive whole number). In Chapter 8, students will revisit the topic of functions in their study of transformations. The rule $(x, y) \rightarrow (x + 5, y - 3)$ defines a function that transforms any point (x, y) in the plane into another unique point.

Chapter 6 first introduces a relation, a rule that, like a function, pairs given inputs with outputs, but without the stipulation that the outputs be unique. The rule "State a number less than the number I name" is a relation because for any given input, there are an infinite number of possible outputs. A function is then defined as a special type of relation for which each input yields exactly one output. The "Add 5" rule given earlier is a function. It assures that an input of 7 yields a unique output, 12.

Chapter 6 introduces several ways of representing functions. These include mapping diagrams, equations, tables of values, and graphs.

A function can be identified graphically using the vertical line test.

If anywhere on the coordinate plane a vertical line intersects the graph in two or more places, the graph is not a function, as shown in Example 2 on the next page. The graph of a linear equation of the form $y = mx + b$ passes the vertical line test, so it represents a linear function.

Much of the focus of Chapter 6 is on algebraic, numerical, and graphical representations of linear functions, along with real-world applications of linear functions. For example, y, the distance traveled by a car traveling for x hours at a rate of 60 miles per hour, is given by the linear function $y = 60x$. The algebraic equation can be used to construct a numerical table of values. The function can be graphed as a line with a slope of 60 and a y-intercept of 0.

At chapter's end, students explore rates of change of functions. If the rate is constant, the function is linear. Its graph is a line with a slope equal to the rate of change. If the rate varies, the function is nonlinear; its graph is something other than a line. Linear and nonlinear functions can be classified as increasing or decreasing.

Identifying Relations and Functions

Relations and functions can be represented by sets of ordered pairs (x, y). The output y is often called the dependent variable, and the input x is called the independent variable. A relation can pair many different y-coordinates with a given x-coordinate, while a function can pair one and only one y-coordinate with a given x-coordinate.

Math Background

Example 1 Representing Relations and Functions as Ordered Pairs

Classify each set of ordered pairs as a relation and/or a function. Explain your reasoning.

A. (4, 5), (3, 6), (0, 9), (4, 7), (5, 9)

B. (1, 3), (2, 2), (7, 5), (9, 5), (6, 6)

Set A is a relation but not a function, because the x-coordinate 4 is paired with two different y-coordinates, 5 and 7. Set B is both a relation and a function. No x-coordinate in set B is paired with more than one y-coordinate.

Example 2 Classifying Real-World Relations and Functions

Classify each situation as a relation and/or a function. Explain your reasoning.

A. independent variable: number of people in a family; dependent variable: number of pets the family has

B. independent variable: number of dimes in your pocket; dependent variable: value of the dimes

Set A is a relation but not a function because it is possible that two families with the same number of people could have two different numbers of pets. So, there could be more than one possible output for a given input. Set B is a relation and a function because a specific number of dimes has one and only one value.

Example 3 Using the Vertical Line Test

Determine if the graph represents a function.

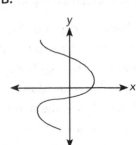

Graph A represents a function because no vertical line intersects the graph in more than one point. Graph B does not represent a function because many vertical lines intersect the graph in more than one point. Two such lines are shown below.

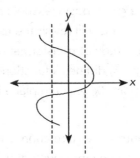

Commentary If students wonder why vertical lines rather than horizontal lines are used to test for functions, remind them of the definition of a function: for every input x, there is only one output y. The points where the vertical line intersects the graph represent all the outputs (y values) that are paired with the input x.

Representing Functions

In Chapter 6, students translate verbal descriptions of functions into equations, tables, and graphs. They learn to analyze and compare functions by translating them into the same form.

Example 4 Translating a Table of Values into a Graph and an Equation

A smoothie machine produces smoothies at a constant rate. The table shows the total volume of smoothies produced, y gallons, as a function of the time the machine has been operating, x minutes. Represent the function with a graph and an equation, and interpret the meaning of the slope and y-intercept of the graph.

Time (x minutes)	0	1	2	3	4
Volume (y gallons)	7	10	13	16	19

Start by graphing the ordered pairs (x, y) represented in the table. Connect the points with a line.

Smoothie Production

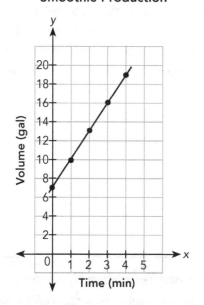

Now use any two points on the graph to write an algebraic equation for the function. To simplify calculations, choose (0, 7) as one of the points and (4, 19) as the other point.

$$\text{Slope } m = \frac{y_2 - y_1}{x_2 - x_1}$$
$$= \frac{19 - 7}{4 - 0}$$
$$= \frac{12}{4}$$
$$= 3$$

Both the table and graph both show the point (0, 7), so $b = 7$. In slope-intercept form, $y = mx + b$, the equation of the line is $y = 3x + 7$.

The y-intercept shows that when someone began counting minutes ($x = 0$), the machine had already produced 7 gallons of smoothies. The slope, 3, indicates that the total volume increased at a rate of 3 gallons per minute.

Commentary Because volume and time are "continuous" quantities, it makes sense to draw a line through the points on the graph in Example 4. Both time and volume can be measured in fractional amounts. Compare this with a discontinuous, or discrete, function like $y = 12x$, where y represents the total cost of x baseball caps selling for $12 apiece. Because it is not possible to buy fractions of caps, the graph must show points only for whole-number values of x.

Understanding Linear and Nonlinear Functions

A linear function involves a constant rate of change, and its graph is a line that can be described by an equation of the form $y = mx + b$. A nonlinear function involves varying rates of change, and its graph is not a line.

Example 5 Using a Table to Identify Linear and Nonlinear Functions

The table shows the volumes of cubes with different edge lengths. Tell whether the table represents a linear or nonlinear function.

Edge length (ft)	1	2	3	4
Volume (ft³)	1	8	27	64

As shown below, numbers can be written above the table to show the changes in input values. Numbers below the table show the changes in output values.

$$+1 \qquad +1 \qquad +1$$

Edge length (ft)	1	2	3	4
Volume (ft³)	1	8	27	64

$$+8 \qquad +19 \qquad +37$$

Rates of change: $\frac{8}{1} = 8$; $\frac{19}{1} = 19$; $\frac{37}{1} = 37$

The rates of change vary, so the function is nonlinear.

Understanding Increasing and Decreasing Functions

If a linear function is increasing, then the rate of change is positive, and the graph of the function rises as you read it from left to right. If a linear function is decreasing, then the rate of change is negative, and the graph falls as you read it from left to right. In Chapter 6, students use graphs to determine whether functions are increasing or decreasing. For linear functions, they also analyze

equations and tables.

Example 6 Classifying Graphs of Functions

Tell whether the function is increasing or decreasing. Then tell whether the function is linear or nonlinear.

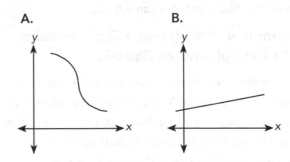

The graph of function A is falling from left to right, so it is decreasing. The graph of function B is rising as you read it from left to right, so it is increasing. Function A is not a line, so it is nonlinear. Function B is a line, so it is linear.

Commentary In Chapter 6, students compare functions quantitatively by comparing their rates of change and their equations, and qualitatively by classifying them as increasing or decreasing. Students also make quick "sketches" of graphs of real-world linear functions. Such graphs are intended to show the output value for an input value of 0 and whether the function is increasing or decreasing.

Additional Teaching Resource

For additional reading, see *The Singapore Model Method for Learning Mathematics* published by the Ministry of Education of Singapore.

Math Background

Additional Teaching Support
- Online Transition Guide
- Online Professional Development Videos

Geometry (G)

Describing and Constructing Figures

Key topics in Course 3 are the Pythagorean Theorem, transformations, congruence, and similarity. Transformations show students yet another way to connect visual representations with algebraic notation, while the lessons on congruence and similarity introduce students to mathematical proofs.

Course 3 builds on development in earlier grades, where students learned to classify angles, triangles, and quadrilaterals.

For example, In Course 2, students explored properties of angle pairs, including angles formed by parallel lines and transversals. They also used geometric properties to produce compass-straightedge constructions. For example, the construction below requires that students know the properties of a parallelogram in order to construct one when given the lengths of two sides and the measure of the included angle.

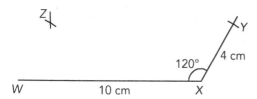

In Course 1, students gained experience locating and describing figures in the coordinate plane. Now, in Course 3, they learn how the Pythagorean Theorem can be used to find the distance between two points in a coordinate system.

Previous work with scale drawings will be applied in Course 3 as students learn to identify similar triangles and find missing side lengths. The concept of scale is also related to transformational geometry, since describing a dilation requires identifying the scale factor.

Solving Real-World and Mathematical Problems

Math in Focus® also provides students with critical opportunities to apply those geometric properties in problem-solving situations or new contexts.

In Courses 1 and 2, students learned to find areas and perimeters of plane figures. They saw that areas can be determined by decomposing polygons into triangles and other shapes. Students solved problems about surfaces areas and volumes of solids. For example, students have learned to find the surface area and the volume of figures such as this one.

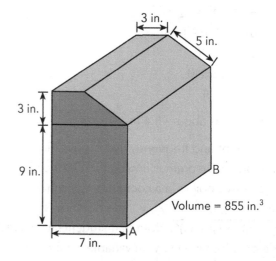

Volume = 855 in.^{3}

In this course, they use the Pythagorean Theorem to solve problems involving dimensions and volumes of solids.

The Pythagorean Theorem

Perhaps no formula in elementary mathematics is included in more courses than the Pythagorean Theorem. Students will use the theorem and its converse in future courses in algebra, geometry, trigonometry, and analysis.

In Course 3, Hands-On Activites give students the opportunity to explain a dissection proof of the theorem and to explore its converse.

They learn that both the theorem and its converse are true, and also that the converse of a theorem is not necessarily true. For example, if a figure is a square, then it has four sides. However, not all figures that have four sides are squares.

Students use the Pythagorean Theorem to determine unknown side lengths in right triangles in both mathematical and real-world problems.

Example 1 Find the Hypotenuse

Jerry takes a diagonal shortcut across a rectangular field that measures 24 meters by 42 meters. About how long is the shortcut?

$$d^2 = 24^2 + 42^2$$
$$d^2 = 576 + 1{,}764$$
$$d^2 = 2{,}340$$
$$d^2 = \sqrt{2{,}340}$$
$$d^2 \approx 48.4$$

The shortcut is about 48.4 meters long.

An important and frequently used application of the Pythagorean Theorem is finding the distance between two points in a coordinate system. For points $A(x_1, y_1)$ and $B(x_2, y_2)$, the distance is $\sqrt{(x_2 - x_1)^2 + (y_2 - y_1)^2}$. Note that students may need some practice working with variables that have subscripts.

Example 2 Use the Distance Formula

Find the distance from $P(2, 4)$ to $Q(-1, -2)$.

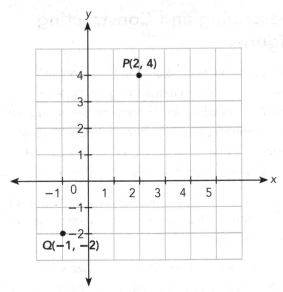

$$PQ = \sqrt{(x_2 - x_1)^2 + (y_2 - y_1)^2}$$
$$= \sqrt{[(-1) - 2]^2 + [(-2) - 4]^2}$$
$$= \sqrt{(-3)^2 + (-6)^2}$$
$$= \sqrt{9 + 36}$$
$$= \sqrt{45}$$

In Course 3, students also practice their spatial reasoning skills by identifying missing dimensions in figures such as rectangular prisms, cones, and pyramids. They use the Pythagorean Theorem to find dimensions that are needed to find volumes of solids.

In future math courses, students will see frequent uses of the Pythagorean Theorem. For example, it will be used to develop the side-length relationships in the 30°-60°-90° and 45°-45°-90° triangles. These relationships play a key role in trigonometry.

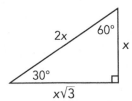

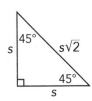

Geometric Transformations

Chapter 8 introduces students to four kinds of transformations: translations, reflections, rotations, and dilations. Students learn how these transformations affect properties of figures such as shape, size, and orientation. They learn that a translation, a reflection, or a rotation results in a figure that is congruent to the original figure, and that a dilation results in a figure that is similar to the original figure.

In Chapter 9 (Congruence and Similarity), students relate what they have learned about transformations to the ideas of congruence and similarity. They learn that a two-dimensional figure is congruent to another if the second can be obtained from the first by a sequence of rotations, reflections, and translations. A transformational definition for similarity is also developed.

Students use paper folding and activities with geometry software to verify experimentally some properties of rotations, reflections, and translations. They also use coordinates to represent transformations as mappings in a coordinate plane. For example, the notation $T(x, y) \rightarrow (x + a, y + b)$ provides an algebraic way to describe a translation.

Example 3 Find Coordinates After Translations

A triangle with vertices at $D(3, -2)$, $E(2, 5)$, and $F(-5, 0)$ is translated 2 units to the left and 3 units down. Find the coordinates of the vertices of the relocated triangle. Then state the new coordinates for any point (x, y) under this translation.

Original Point	Is Mapped Onto
$D(3, -2)$	$D'(1, -5)$
$E(2, 5)$	$E'(0, 2)$
$F(-5, 0)$	$F'(-7, -3)$
(x, y)	$(x - 2, y - 3)$

To create the mapping diagram in Example 3, students learn to apply the transformation $T(x, y) \rightarrow (x - 2, y - 3)$ to each point. They use both mapping tables and also drawings on coordinate grids to represent transformations.

Example 4 Find the Center of Dilation

The table lists the vertices of a triangle and their corresponding images. The points are mapped onto their images by a dilation. Draw the triangle and its image. Label point P as the center of dilation.

Original Point	$A(1, -2)$	$B(4, -1)$	$C(5, -3)$
Is Mapped Onto	$A'(0, 1)$	$B'(6, 3)$	$C'(8, -1)$

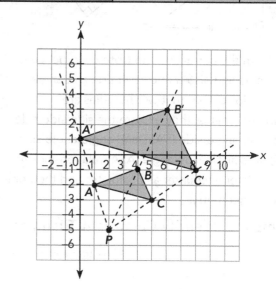

A is joined to A' and B is joined to B'. The lines intersect at P, the center of the dilation.

Commentary In a problem such as Example 4, students can apply the distance formula they learned in Chapter 7 to find the scale factor. Computing the ratio of any pair of corresponding sides shows that the scale factor is 2.

Congruence and Similarity

In previous grades students have identified congruent and similar figures using informal descriptions such as "same size and shape" or "same shape but not necessarily same size." In Chapter 9, students learn more precise ways to determine congruence and similarity. They begin by identifying corresponding sides and angles in a pair of congruent triangles.

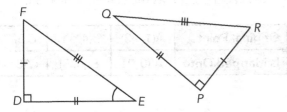

They learn the correct way to write congruence statements and also that certain side and angle relationships ensure that two triangles are congruent. That is, they explore the side-side-side (SSS), side-angle-side (SAS), and angle-angle-side (AAS), and angle-side angle (ASA) relationships that they will later encounter as postulates and theorems in formal geometry.

Example 5 Identify Congruent Triangles

Identify the congruent triangles. Write a statement of congruence and state the test used.

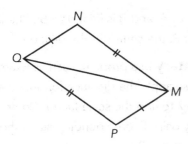

Statement of congruence: $\triangle NQM \equiv \triangle PMQ$ by the SSS test. $QN = MP$, $QP = MN$, and $QM = QM$ because it is a common side of the triangles.

To test for similarity in a pair of triangles, students establish that two triangles are similar if two angles in one are congruent to two angles in the other (AA). They also learn that triangles are similar if they have three pairs of corresponding sides with the same ratio, or two pairs of corresponding sides with the same ratio and included angles that are congruent. They use similarity concepts to solve problems like the one in Example 6.

Example 6 Find Unknown Measures in Similar Figures

Alex drew this figure to find the distance d across a pond. Explain why the triangles are similar. Then find the distance across the pond.

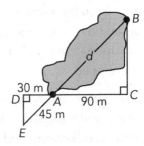

The triangles are similar because of the angle-angle test. AD is $\frac{1}{3}$ of AC, so AE must be $\frac{1}{3}$ of AB.

$$45 = \frac{1}{3}d$$
$$3 \cdot 45 = d$$
$$d = 135$$

The distance across the pond is 135 meters.

Additional Teaching Resource

For additional reading, see *The Singapore Model Method for Learning Mathematics* published by the Ministry of Education of Singapore.

Statistics and Probability (SP)

Analyzing Bivariate Data

From Grade 3 through Course 2, students have organized and analyzed data in a variety of displays, including line plots, line graphs, dot plots, frequency tables, histograms, and box-and-whisker plots. All of these data displays are appropriate for analyzing univariate data, or data containing one variable.

In Course 3, students use their data analysis skills to draw conclusions about bivariate data, or data containing two variables. Students learn to observe the simultaneous measurement of two characteristics represented by variables. These variables can take on quantitative (numerical) values or qualitative (categorical) values.

Students learn to use scatter plots to represent and analyze quantitative, bivariate data. If there is a strong linear association between the two data sets, a line of best fit can be drawn. Then students use two points on the line to find its slope and then write an equation for the line in slope-intercept form. The equation can be used to make estimates or predictions about the data.

To analyze qualitative, bivariate data, students use two-way tables. These tables are an extension of the frequency tables used in Course 1 to summarize the results of univariate data collected from surveys. Now, the tables contain two variables with categorical values, so students must consider the occurrences of each data combination.

Probability of Compound Events

Probability of simple events is explored in Grades 4 and 5. In Course 2, students learn to define outcomes and find the probability of simple events. They also use Venn diagrams to represent two types of compound events: mutually exclusive and non-mutually exclusive events. The primary focus is on finding the probability of the events involved in such compound events.

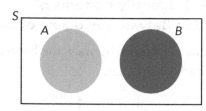

Events *A* and *B* are mutually exclusive.

Course 3 focuses on the probability of other types of compound events. First, students use possibility diagrams, such as two-way tables and tree diagrams, to find the probability of compound events. Then, independent and dependent events are introduced as types of compound events. Students find the probability of independent and dependent events using the multiplication rule of probability. They also find the probability of mutually exclusive events using the addition rule of probability.

Math Background

Quantitative Data

While analyzing dot plots of univariate data in Course 1, students learned that the shape formed by the dots is significant. Now they learn that the arrangement of data points in a scatter plot of bivariate data has special meaning. Data points that cluster in a predictable pattern show a strong association, which may also have a positive or negative association and a linear or nonlinear association. A line of best fit is used to describe data with a strong linear correlation.

Example 1 Identify Patterns of Association Between Two Sets of Data

Describe the association between the bivariate data shown in each scatter plot.

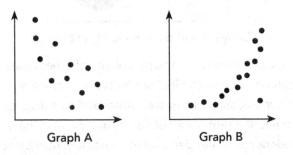

Graph A	Graph B
The data show a weak association.	The data show a strong, nonlinear association.

Commentary Students should be aware that data points in a scatter plot don't need to follow an exact pattern to have a strong association. As long as most of the data points are close to each other and follow a general pattern, the data have a strong association, even if there are outliers.

Example 2 Use a Linear Equation to Describe Bivariate Quantitative Data

Make a scatter plot and sketch a line of best fit for the data below. Write an equation of the line of best fit.

At Bats	73	70	36	53	48	63	42
Hits	22	28	10	15	12	19	11

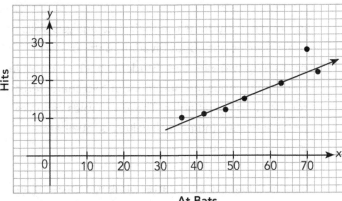

At Bats and Hits

Use the fact that the line passes through points (42, 11) and (63, 19) to find the slope of the line.

$$m = \frac{19 - 11}{63 - 42} = \frac{8}{21} \approx 0.38$$

Then find the y-intercept by using a point on the line and the slope-intercept equation $y = mx + b$.

$$11 = 0.38(42) + b$$
$$-4.96 = b$$

An equation of the line is $y = 0.38x - 4.96$.

Commentary Although students will learn in a later course how to use algebraic methods to find a line of best fit, the process they apply at this level leads to subjective results. To help insure that students' lines describe the data as accurately as possible, emphasize that there should be about as many points above the line as below it.

Math Background

Qualitative Data

A two-way table is used to organize bivariate data with categorical values. The values of one categorical variable are used as column heads and the values of the other variable are used as row heads. The number of occurrences of each data pair is written in the corresponding table cell. It is helpful to calculate the relative frequency of each data pair. The relative frequency can be thought of as the percent of time that data combination occurs in the category.

Example 3 Convert Data to Relative Frequencies in a Two-way Table

The two-way table shows the admission tickets sold at a science museum during one day.

Admission Ticket Type

		Exhibitions	Planetarium	Total
Age	Child	122	62	184
	Adult	96	140	236
	Total	218	202	420

Find the relative frequencies to compare the distribution of the ages among each admission ticket sales. Describe the distributions.

Admission Ticket Type

		Exhibitions	Planetarium
Age	Child	$\frac{122}{218} \approx 0.56$	$\frac{62}{202} \approx 0.31$
	Adult	$\frac{96}{218} \approx 0.44$	$\frac{140}{202} \approx 0.69$
	Total	1	1

For the exhibition halls, there were more child tickets sold than adult tickets. For the planetarium, there were more adult tickets sold than child tickets.

Using Possibility Diagrams

Students can use two-way tables and tree diagrams to find the probabilities of compound events by counting the number of favorable outcomes and the total number of outcomes.

A tree diagram uses branches to show all possible outcomes. The probability of each outcome is written along the branch. If all of the outcomes are equally likely, as in the example below, then the probabilities are not labeled on the branches.

Example 4 Use Tree Diagrams to Find Probability of Compound Events

Two fair coins are tossed together. Draw a tree diagram to represent the possible outcomes. Then use it to find the probability of getting tails on at least one coin.

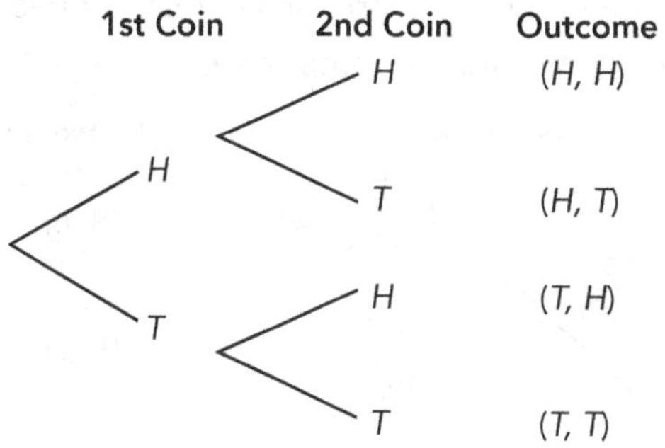
1st Coin
2nd Coin
Outcome
H
T
H
T
H
T
(H, H)
(H, T)
(T, H)
(T, T)

H represents heads, *T* represents tails

The probability of (*H*, *T*), (*T*, *H*) or (*T*, *T*) is $\frac{3}{4}$. So, $P(\text{tails on at least one coin}) = \frac{3}{4}$.

Using Rules to Find Probabilities

Independent events are compound events in which the probability of one event does not affect the probability of the other event. For two such events, the probability that both occur is the product of the probabilities of the events (multiplication rule of probability).

Mutually exclusive events are compound events that have no common outcomes. For two mutually exclusive events, the probability that either of the events occurs is the sum of the probabilities of the events (addition rule of probability).

Example 5 Solve Probability Problems Involving Compound Events

A bag contains 7 blue marbles and 3 yellow marbles. Two marbles are randomly drawn, one at a time with replacement. Find the probability that the two marbles drawn are the same color.

1st Draw   2nd Draw   Outcome

B represents blue, Y represents yellow

$$P(B, B) \text{ or } P(Y, Y) = P(B) \cdot P(B) + P(Y) \cdot P(Y)$$
$$= \frac{7}{10} \cdot \frac{7}{10} + \frac{3}{10} \cdot \frac{3}{10}$$
$$= \frac{58}{100}$$

Dependent events are compound events in which the probability of one event affects the probability of the other. For two such events, the probability that both events occur is the product of the probability of the first event and the conditional probability of the second event given the first (multiplication rule of probability).

Example 6 Solve a Probability Problem Involving Dependent Events

A class has 13 female students and 11 male students. Two students are picked randomly, one at a time without replacement. Find the probability of picking a female student and then a male student.

1st Pick   2nd Pick   Outcome

F represents female, M represents male

$$P(F, M) = P(F) \cdot P(M \text{ after } F)$$
$$= \frac{13}{24} \cdot \frac{11}{23}$$
$$= \frac{143}{552}$$

Additional Teaching Resource

For additional reading, see *The Singapore Model Method for Learning Mathematics* published by the Ministry of Education of Singapore.

Interpret the Real Number System

TEACHING STRATEGY

1. **Vocabulary** Make sure students understand the terms *real number*, *rational number*, *irrational number*, *non-integer*, *terminating decimal*, *repeating decimal*, *integer*, *negative integer*, *whole number*, *positive integer*, and *zero*. Point out that the set of real numbers includes several smaller classifications of numbers.

2. **Teach** Direct students to the diagram. **Ask** What numbers make up the whole numbers? [zero and positive integers] What numbers make up the integers? [negative integers and whole numbers] What numbers make up the rational numbers? [non-integers and integers] What numbers make up the real numbers? [rational numbers and irrational numbers] Direct students to the example. **Ask** Why is 11 listed as a whole number, an integer, and a rational number? [All whole numbers are integers and rational numbers.] Why is –2 listed as an integer and a rational number? [All integers are rational numbers.]

3. **Quick Check** Look for these common errors.
   - Forgetting to identify whole numbers and integers as rational numbers.
   - Failing to understand the difference between rational and irrational numbers.

4. **Next Steps** Assign the practice exercises. For students who need more support, use the alternate teaching strategy.

Additional Teaching Resource

Online Transition Guide with Reteach and Extra Practice worksheets from previous grade levels

ALTERNATE INTERVENTION STRATEGY

Materials: none

Strategy: Use a Venn diagram to classify real numbers.

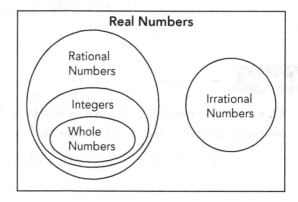

1. Remind students that a Venn Diagram is a way of visually organizing sets that may overlap. Direct them to the Venn diagram on the board. **Ask** Which set of numbers includes the fewest numbers? [whole numbers] Which set of numbers includes the most numbers? [real numbers]

2. Point out that the set of Whole Numbers is inside Integers, which is inside Rational Numbers, which is inside Real Numbers. **Ask** What does this mean with respect to the number 1? [It is a whole number, an integer, a rational number, and a real number.]

3. **Ask** Why is the section for Irrational Numbers by itself? [Rational numbers and irrational numbers have no numbers in common. Together they make up the real numbers.]

4. Write the following on the board: 0, –3, $\frac{6}{7}$, $\sqrt{8}$, –5.2, $7\frac{1}{4}$, 1.5934..., 9, 0.4. Have students identify every group to which each number belongs based on the way the sections of the Venn diagram are nested.

Interpret the Real Number System

The diagram shows the relationships among numbers in the real number system.

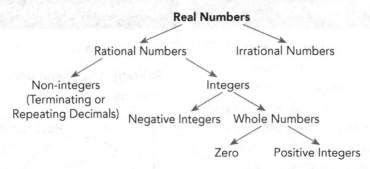

Example

Classify the numbers listed as whole numbers, integers, rational numbers, or irrational numbers. Each number may be in more than one classification.

$11, -2, \frac{2}{3}, 14, 0.8, 3, \sqrt{10}, 1\frac{3}{4}, 0.777..., \sqrt{3}, 5, \frac{6}{5}, 0.34519..., 0, 1.95, -30, \sqrt[3]{12}$

Whole Numbers	11, 14, 3, 5, 0
Integers	11, –2, 14, 3, 5, 0, –30
Rational Numbers	$11, -2, \frac{2}{3}, 14, 0.8, 3, 1\frac{3}{4}, 0.777..., 5, \frac{6}{5}, 0, 1.95, -30$
Irrational Numbers	$\sqrt{10}, \sqrt{3}, 0.34519..., \sqrt[3]{12}$

✓ Quick Check
Use the list of numbers below.

$$0.3939..., \sqrt{45}, 9, -2$$

1 Identify the irrational numbers. _____

2 Identify the whole numbers. _____

3 Identify the rational numbers. _____

4 Identify the integers. _____

Practice on Your Own
Use the list of numbers below.

$$13, \sqrt{32}, -4, 2.3, \frac{14}{5}, 0, \sqrt{100}, 0.1936..., 1\frac{5}{7}$$

5 Identify the integers. _____

6 Identify the rational numbers. _____

7 Identify the whole numbers. _____

8 Identify the irrational numbers. _____

NS SKILL 2 Write Terminating or Repeating Decimals

TEACHING STRATEGY

1. **Vocabulary** Make sure students understand the terms *terminating decimal* and *repeating decimal*. Remind them that *terminate* means "to come to an end." So if the division ends, the decimal terminates, and if the division does not end, the decimal repeats.

2. **Teach** Direct students to Step 1 of Example 1. **Ask** Which number is the dividend? [3] The divisor? [4] Direct students to Step 2. **Ask** Where do you place the decimal point in the quotient? [directly above the decimal point in the dividend] Direct students to Step 3. Explain that you can insert as many zeros at the end of the dividend as you need to complete the division. Lead students through Steps 1 and 2 of Example 2. Direct students to Step 3. **Ask** Which digit repeats in the quotient? [3] Explain that a bar is drawn above the repeating digit or digits. Tell students that a decimal can begin to repeat at any time after the decimal point, and that any number of digits may repeat.

3. **Quick Check** Look for these common errors.
   - Mistakenly dividing the denominator by the numerator instead of the numerator by the denominator.
   - Not dividing to enough places to determine whether a quotient is a terminating or repeating decimal.
   - Drawing a bar over all the digits after the decimal point, even though not all of those digits repeat.

4. **Next Steps** Assign the practice exercises. For students who need more support, use the alternate teaching strategy.

Additional Teaching Resource

 Online Transition Guide with Reteach and Extra Practice worksheets from previous grade levels

ALTERNATE INTERVENTION STRATEGY

Materials: calculator

Strategy: Use a calculator to find a decimal for a rational number.

1. Write the fraction $\frac{7}{8}$ on the board. Remind students that the fraction bar represents a division sign, so $\frac{7}{8} = 7 \div 8$. Have students use a calculator to divide 7 by 8. **Ask** What is the quotient? [0.875] Is the decimal a terminating decimal or a repeating decimal? [terminating decimal] How do you know? [There are no digits that repeat.] On the board write $\frac{7}{8} = 0.875$.

2. Write the fraction $\frac{5}{12}$ on the board. Have students use a calculator to divide 5 by 12. **Ask** What quotient is displayed on the calculator? [0.4166666667] Are there any digits that repeat? [Yes.] What digit repeats? [6] Is the decimal a terminating decimal or a repeating decimal? [repeating decimal] Explain that a calculator can only display a specific number of decimal places, so the last digit on the display is sometimes rounded up. The digit 7 that appears in 0.4166666667 is an example of this. **Ask** How can you represent the digit that repeats? [Draw a bar over it.] On the board write $\frac{5}{12} = 0.41\overline{6}$.

3. Have students use a calculator to find decimals for the following rational numbers: $\frac{4}{5}, \frac{2}{3}, \frac{3}{8}, \frac{2}{9}, \frac{7}{11}, \frac{11}{15}$, and $\frac{13}{20}$. Have students tell which are terminating decimals and which are repeating decimals.

Write Terminating or Repeating Decimals

Example 1 | Terminating Decimal

Write $\frac{3}{4}$ as a decimal.

STEP 1 Divide the numerator by the denominator.

$$\frac{3}{4} \rightarrow 4\overline{)3}$$

STEP 2 In the dividend, insert a decimal point followed by zeros. In the space where the quotient will go, place a decimal point directly above the decimal point in the dividend.

$$4\overline{)3.00}$$

STEP 3 Divide. If you eventually get a remainder of 0, the decimal terminates.

$$
\begin{array}{r}
0.75 \\
4\overline{)3.00} \\
-28 \\
\hline
20 \\
-20 \\
\hline
0
\end{array}
$$

So, $\frac{3}{4} = 0.75$.

Example 2 | Repeating Decimal

Write $\frac{5}{6}$ as a decimal.

STEP 1 Divide the numerator by the denominator.

$$\frac{5}{6} \rightarrow 6\overline{)5}$$

STEP 2 In the dividend, insert a decimal point followed by zeros. In the space where the quotient will go, place a decimal point directly above the decimal point in the dividend.

$$6\overline{)5.000}$$

STEP 3 Divide. If the remainders start to repeat, the decimal repeats.

$$
\begin{array}{r}
0.833 \\
6\overline{)5.000} \\
-48 \\
\hline
20 \\
-18 \\
\hline
20 \\
-18 \\
\hline
2
\end{array}
$$

So, $\frac{5}{6} = 0.833...$ or $0.8\overline{3}$.

✔ Quick Check

Write each number as a terminating or repeating decimal.

1 $\frac{2}{5}$ _____

2 $\frac{5}{8}$ _____

3 $\frac{3}{11}$ _____

4 $\frac{19}{12}$ _____

Practice on Your Own
Write each number as a terminating or repeating decimal.

5 $\frac{9}{20}$ _____

6 $\frac{13}{15}$ _____

7 $\frac{5}{9}$ _____

8 $\frac{57}{40}$ _____

9 $1\frac{1}{2}$ _____

10 $2\frac{11}{12}$ _____

Locate Irrational Numbers on a Number Line

TEACHING STRATEGY

1. **Vocabulary** Make sure students understand the term *irrational number*. Remind them that an irrational number may be the square root of a number that is not a perfect square, or the cube root of a number that is not a perfect cube. An irrational number does not terminate or repeat when written as a decimal.

2. **Teach** Direct students to Step 1 of Example 1. **Ask** What two perfect squares does 21 lie between? [16 and 25] Is 21 closer to 16 or 25? [It is about halfway between 16 and 25.] What decimal is halfway between 4 and 5? [4.5] Have students find 4.5^2 to verify that it is about 21. Direct students to Step 2. Point out that $\sqrt{21}$ has been plotted on the number line at about 4.5. Direct students to Step 1 of Example 2. **Ask** What two perfect cubes does 30 lie between? [27 and 64] Is 30 closer to 27 or 64? [27] What decimal is an approximate value of $\sqrt[3]{30}$? [3.1] Have students find $(3.1)^3$ to verify that it is about 30. Direct students to Step 2. Point out that $\sqrt[3]{30}$ has been plotted on the number line at about 3.1.

3. **Quick Check** Look for these common errors.
   • Incorrectly approximating the square root or cube root.
   • Incorrectly locating a point on the number line.

4. **Next Steps** Assign the practice exercises to students. For students who need more support, use the alternate teaching strategy.

Additional Teaching Resource

🖲 Online Transition Guide with Reteach and Extra Practice worksheets from previous grade levels

ALTERNATE INTERVENTION STRATEGY

Materials: calculator, TRT1 (Number Lines)

Strategy: Use a calculator to find the approximate value of an irrational number.

1. Have students locate the square root key on their calculators. This key is usually designated by $\sqrt{\square}$ or $\sqrt{x}$.

2. Write $\sqrt{8}$ on the board. Have students use a calculator to find $\sqrt{8}$. **Ask** What answer is displayed on the calculator? [2.828427125]

3. Review how to round a number to the nearest tenth with students. **Ask** What is the tenths digit? [8] What is the hundredths digit? [2] Is the hundredths digit less than 5 or greater than or equal to 5? [less than 5] Do you round up or down if the digit is less than 5? [down] What is $\sqrt{8}$ rounded to the nearest tenth? [2.8]

4. Have students find 2.8^2 by using the calculator. **Ask** What is the result? [7.84] Is 7.84 close to 8? [Yes.] Tell students that the square root of 8 is about 2.8.

5. Draw a number line on the board. Have a volunteer plot $\sqrt{8}$ on the number line at about 2.8.

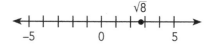

6. Have students use a calculator to find the approximate value of more irrational numbers and locate them on a number line.

Name _____ Date _____

Locate Irrational Numbers on a Number Line

An irrational number cannot be written as a ratio of two integers.

When written as a decimal, an irrational number does not terminate or repeat.

If you approximate the value of an irrational number, you can locate it on a number line.

Example 1

Locate $\sqrt{21}$ on a number line.

STEP 1   Identify the perfect squares that 21 lies between.
$$4^2 = 16$$
$$5^2 = 25$$

21 is about halfway between 16 and 25, so the value of $\sqrt{21}$ is about 4.5.

STEP 2   Draw a number line.
Plot $\sqrt{21}$ at about 4.5.

Example 2

Locate $\sqrt[3]{30}$ on a number line.

STEP 1   Identify the perfect cubes that 30 lies between.
$$3^3 = 27$$
$$4^3 = 64$$

30 is much closer to 27 than to 64, so the value of $\sqrt[3]{30}$ is closer to 3 than to 4.

STEP 2   Draw a number line.
Plot $\sqrt[3]{30}$ closer to 3 than to 4.

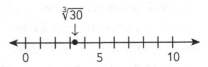

✔ Quick Check

**Find a rational approximation for each irrational number.
Then locate the number on the number line.**

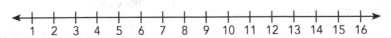

1 $\sqrt{10}$ _____   **2** $\sqrt{40}$ _____   **3** $\sqrt[3]{22}$ _____

Practice on Your Own

**Find a rational approximation for each irrational number.
Then locate the number on the number line.**

4 $\sqrt{29}$ _____   **5** $\sqrt{56}$ _____   **6** $\sqrt[3]{75}$ _____

Add Integers

TEACHING STRATEGY

1. **Vocabulary** Make sure students understand the terms *positive integer*, *negative integer*, and *absolute value*. Remind them that the absolute value of a number is the distance from 0 to that number on a number line.

2. **Teach** Direct students to Example 1. In Step 1, have them look at the intervals marked on the number line. **Ask** Which direction is the positive direction? [to the right] Which direction is the negative direction? [to the left] Tell students to start at 0, move 4 units to the right, and then 9 units to the left. **Ask** At what point do you finish? [–5] On the board write 4 + (–9) = –5. Direct students to Example 2. Point out that the signs are different: one sign is positive, and one sign is negative. **Ask** According to the rules, what do we first do to add integers with different signs? [Subtract the absolute values of the integers.] Tell students to ignore the signs and subtract the smaller absolute value from the larger absolute value. **Ask** Which number has the greater absolute value? [–9] What will the sign of the sum be? [negative]

3. **Quick Check** Look for these common errors.
   • Moving in the wrong direction on the number line.
   • When using the rules, choosing an incorrect sign for the sum.

4. **Next Steps** Assign the practice exercises. For students who need more support, use the alternate teaching strategy.

Additional Teaching Resource
Online Transition Guide with Reteach and Extra Practice worksheets from previous grade levels

ALTERNATE INTERVENTION STRATEGY

Materials: colored counters

Strategy: Use counters to add integers.

1. Give students two sets of colored counters. Tell them that one color represents positive integers and the other color represents negative integers.

2. Have students model –8 + 3 with the counters.

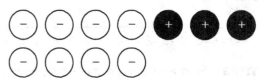

3. Explain that one positive counter and one negative counter together make a zero pair because 1 + (–1) = 0. Have students move counters to form as many zero pairs as possible. Tell them that zero pairs can be removed because the pairs of negative and positive counters cancel each other out.

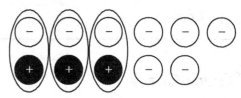

4. **Ask** How many counters are left over? [5 negative counters] What number do the left over counters represent? [–5] On the board write –8 + 3 = –5.

5. Have students use the counters to find the sums of other pairs of integers. Be sure to include sums of two positive integers, sums of two negative integers, and sums of a positive integer and a negative integer.

Add Integers

Name _____   Date _____

You can use a number line or the following rules to add integers.

Add integers with the same sign.	Add the absolute values. Keep the same sign.
Add integers with different signs.	Subtract the absolute values. Use the sign of the number with the greater absolute value.

Example 1 Number line

Add 4 + (–9).

STEP 1 Draw a number line.

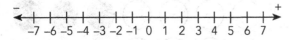

STEP 2 Start at 0. Since 4 is positive, move 4 units to the right. From that point, move 9 units to the left since –9 is negative.
The final location is –5.

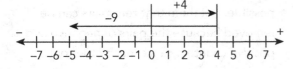

So, 4 + (–9) = –5.

Example 2 Rules for addition

Add 4 + (–9).

STEP 1 Identify whether the signs are the same or different.
The signs are different.

STEP 2 Find the absolute values.
$$|4| = 4 \qquad |-9| = 9$$
Subtract: 9 – 4 = 5

STEP 3 Use the sign of the number with the greater absolute value.
The absolute value of 9 is greater than the absolute value of 4, so the sign will be negative.

So, 4 + (–9) = –5.

✔ Quick Check
Evaluate.

1 –2 + (–5) _____

2 7 + (–9) _____

3 –6 + 7 _____

Practice on Your Own
Evaluate.

4 –5 + 8 _____

5 –3 + (–3) _____

6 7 + (–2) _____

7 2 + (–9) _____

8 7 + (–10) _____

9 –4 + 4 _____

10 –7 + 13 _____

11 –2 + (–2) _____

12 –5 + 10 _____

13 –1 + 5 + 3 _____

14 –3 + (–1) + (–2) _____

15 –1 + 8 + (–7) _____

NS
SKILL 5 Subtract Integers

<table>
<tr><td>

TEACHING STRATEGY

</td><td>

ALTERNATE INTERVENTION STRATEGY

</td></tr>
<tr><td>

1. **Vocabulary** Make sure students understand the terms *positive integer*, *negative integer*, and *opposite*. Remind them that addition and subtraction are inverse operations.

2. **Teach** Direct students to Step 1 of Example 1. **Ask** Which numbers are to the right? [positive] Which numbers are to the left? [negative] Direct students to Step 2 of Example 1. Tell students to start at 0. **Ask** To find –2 – (–6), in which direction will you move first, and how many units will you move? [2 units left] Direct students to Step 3. **Ask** What is the sign of the second number? [negative] Tell students that, since the number being subtracted is negative, you move to the right. **Ask** How many units will you move to the right? [6] At what point do you end? [4] On the board write –2 – (–6) = 4. Direct students to Step 1 of Example 2. **Ask** What is the rule for subtracting integers? [Add the opposite of the number being subtracted.] Tell students to follow the rules for addition in Steps 2–4.

3. **Quick Check** Look for these common errors.
   • Moving in the wrong direction on a number line when subtracting.
   • When using the rule, forgetting to change the sign of the second integer.

4. **Next Steps** Assign the practice exercises. For students who need more support, use the alternate teaching strategy.

</td><td>

Materials: colored counters

Strategy: Use counters to subtract integers.

1. Give students two sets of colored counters. One color represents positive integers and the other color negative integers.

2. Have students use the counters to find 3 – (–2). Tell students to model the first integer, 3.

3. **Ask** Do you have enough counters to subtract the second number? [No, there are no negative counters in the model.] Explain that it is necessary to add zero pairs to the model of the first integer so that there are enough counters to take away. Since you are going to have to eventually remove 2 negative counters, you should add 2 zero pairs. Point out that adding zero pairs does not change the value of the original number.

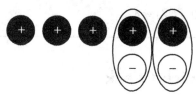

4. **Ask** Do you have enough counters to subtract the second integer? [Yes.] Take away 2 negative counters.

5. **Ask** How many counters are left? [5 positive counters] On the board write 3 – (–2) = 5.

6. Have students use the counters to find the differences of other pairs of integers.

</td></tr>
</table>

Additional Teaching Resource
🖱 Online Transition Guide with Reteach and Extra Practice worksheets from previous grade levels

NS
SKILL 5 # Subtract Integers

You can use a number line or the following rule to subtract two integers.
To subtract two integers, add the opposite of the number being subtracted.

Example 1 | **Number line**

Subtract −2 − (−6).

STEP 1 Draw a number line.

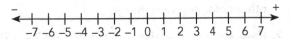

STEP 2 Start at 0. Since −2 is negative, move 2 units to the left.

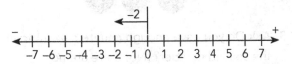

STEP 3 Subtracting −6 is the same as adding 6. From −2, move 6 units to the right. The final location is 4.

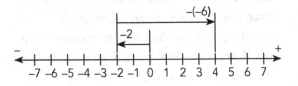

So, −2 − (−6) = 4.

Example 2 | **Rule for subtraction**

Subtract −2 − (−6).

STEP 1 Rewrite the problem as an addition problem by adding the opposite of −6. The opposite of −6 is 6.
$$-2 - (-6) = -2 + 6$$

STEP 2 Identify whether the signs are the same or different.
The signs are different.

STEP 3 Find the absolute values.
$$|-2| = 2 \qquad |6| = 6$$
Subtract: 6 − 2 = 4

STEP 4 Use the sign of the number with the greater absolute value.
The absolute value of 6 is greater than the absolute value of −2, so the sign will be positive.

So, −2 − (−6) = 4.

☑ **Quick Check**
Evaluate.

1 1 − 5 _____

2 4 − (−2) _____

3 −3 − 2 _____

Practice on Your Own
Evaluate.

4 −5 − 2 _____

5 −3 − (−3) _____

6 2 − (−4) _____

7 2 − 9 _____

8 −7 − (−10) _____

9 −1 − 3 _____

10 6 − 5 − 7 _____

11 2 − (−2) − 8 _____

12 −6 − (−8) − 2 _____

13 5 − 9 − (−9) _____

14 18 − 19 − 1 _____

15 −3 − (−3) − 3 _____

Multiply Integers

TEACHING STRATEGY	ALTERNATE INTERVENTION STRATEGY

TEACHING STRATEGY

1. **Vocabulary** Make sure students understand the terms *positive integer*, *negative integer*, and *product*.

2. **Teach** Direct students to Step 1 of Example 1. **Ask** What is the sign of –4? [negative] What is the sign of –5? [negative] Are the signs the same or different? [the same] What is the rule for multiplying two integers with the same sign? [If the signs are the same, the product will be positive.] Direct students to Step 2. **Ask** What is 4 times 5? [20] So, what is the product of –4 and –5? [20] Direct students to Step 1 of Example 2. **Ask** What is the sign of –6? [negative] What is the sign of 3? [positive] Are the signs the same or different? [different] What is the rule for multiplying two integers with different signs? [If the signs are different, the product will be negative.] Direct students to Step 2. **Ask** What is 6 times 3? [18] And since the product must be negative, what is the product of $-6 \cdot 3$? [–18]

3. **Quick Check** Look for these common errors.
   • Adding or subtracting the integers instead of multiplying.
   • Using the wrong sign for the product.

4. **Next Steps** Assign the practice exercises. For students who need more support, use the alternate teaching strategy.

Additional Teaching Resource
Online Transition Guide with Reteach and Extra Practice worksheets from previous grade levels

ALTERNATE INTERVENTION STRATEGY

Materials: TRT48 (Integer Multiplication Flashcards)

Strategy: Students use flashcards to practice multiplying integers.

1. Assign or have students select partners. Distribute one deck of cards to each pair.

2. Have students separate the cards into two groups: one group with expressions that show positive and negative signs only, and one group with expressions that include integers.

3. Tell students to shuffle the group of cards with expressions that feature signs only. Students should take turns drawing a card and stating the rule for the card. When they have stated the rule for the card, have them write the sign of the product on the back of the card.

4. When students show an understanding of the rules, tell them to switch to the cards with the integers.

5. Have students shuffle the cards with the integer expressions. Students should take turns drawing a card.

6. For each card drawn, the student should first state the rule that determines the sign of the product of the integers. Then he or she must evaluate the expression and state the product. Students may use pencil and paper, if needed.

7. If the student gets the product correct, he or she gets to keep the card. If not the card is returned to the deck. Play alternates until all of the expressions have been correctly evaluated. In each pair, the student with the most cards at the end of the game is the winner.

Name _____ Date _____

Multiply Integers

When you multiply two integers with the **same sign**, the product is **positive**.	$(+) \cdot (+) = (+)$ $(-) \cdot (-) = (+)$
When you multiply two integers with **different signs**, the product is **negative**.	$(+) \cdot (-) = (-)$ $(-) \cdot (+) = (-)$

Example 1 **Same sign**

Multiply $(-4) \cdot (-5)$.

STEP 1 First determine the sign of the product.
$$(-) \cdot (-) = (+)$$
The signs are the same, so the product will be positive.

STEP 2 Multiply as you would with whole numbers.
$$4 \cdot 5 = 20$$

So, $(-4) \cdot (-5) = 20$.

Example 2 **Different signs**

Multiply $(-6) \cdot 3$.

STEP 1 First determine the sign of the product.
$$(-) \cdot (+) = (-)$$
The signs are different, so the product will be negative.

STEP 2 Multiply as you would with whole numbers.
$$6 \cdot 3 = 18$$

So, $(-6) \cdot 3 = -18$.

✔ Quick Check
Evaluate.

1 $2 \cdot (-7)$ _____

2 $(-8) \cdot (-3)$ _____

3 $(-9) \cdot 4$ _____

Practice on Your Own
Evaluate.

4 $(-2) \cdot (-5)$ _____

5 $3 \cdot (-9)$ _____

6 $(-4) \cdot (-8)$ _____

7 $13 \cdot (-1)$ _____

8 $7 \cdot 4$ _____

9 $(-8) \cdot 9$ _____

10 $(-15) \cdot 0$ _____

11 $5 \cdot (-9)$ _____

12 $(-6) \cdot (-6)$ _____

13 $5 \cdot (-6) \cdot (-2)$ _____

14 $(-2) \cdot (-4) \cdot (-5)$ _____

15 $(-6) \cdot 1 \cdot (-8)$ _____

Divide Integers

TEACHING STRATEGY

1. **Vocabulary** Make sure students understand the terms *positive integer*, *negative integer*, and *quotient*.

2. **Teach** Direct students to Step 1 of Example 1. **Ask** What is the sign of –36? [negative] What is the sign of –4? [negative] Are the signs the same or different? [the same] What is the rule for dividing two integers with the same sign? [If the signs are the same, the quotient will be positive.] Direct students to Step 2. **Ask** What is 36 divided by 4? [9] So, what is the quotient? [9] Direct students to Step 1 of Example 2. **Ask** What is the sign of 40? [positive] What is the sign of –5? [negative] Are the signs the same or different? [different] What is the rule for dividing two integers with different signs? [If the signs are different, the quotient will be negative.] Direct students to Step 2. **Ask** What is 40 divided by 5? [8] So, what is the quotient? [–8]

3. **Quick Check** Look for these common errors.
   - Adding, subtracting, or multiplying the integers instead of dividing.
   - Using the wrong sign for the quotient.

4. **Next Steps** Assign the practice exercises. For students who need more support, use the alternate teaching strategy.

Additional Teaching Resource

Online Transition Guide with Reteach and Extra Practice worksheets from previous grade levels

ALTERNATE INTERVENTION STRATEGY

Materials: none

Strategy: Divide integers by writing a related multiplication sentence.

1. Explain that multiplication and division are inverse operations. They undo each other. Tell students that every multiplication sentence with nonzero factors has two related division sentences. **Ask** What are the related division sentences for $6 \cdot 5 = 30$? [$30 \div 6 = 5$ and $30 \div 5 = 6$]

2. Write the following table on the board.

$6 \cdot (-5) = -30$	$(-6) \cdot (-5) = 30$	$(-6) \cdot 5 = -30$
$(-30) \div 6 =$ __	$30 \div (-6) =$ __	$(-30) \div (-6) =$ __
$(-30) \div (-5) =$ __	$30 \div (-5) =$ __	$(-30) \div 5 =$ __

Have students fill in the chart, completing the related division sentences for each multiplication sentence. [Row 2: –5, –5, 5; Row 3: 6, –6, –6]

3. After students have completed the chart, have them complete the following statements.

$24 \div (-3) =$ _____ because $(-3) \cdot$ _____ $= 24$.

$(-28) \div 4 =$ _____ because $4 \cdot$ _____ $= -28$.

$(-15) \div (-5) =$ _____ because $(-5) \cdot$ _____ $= -15$.

4. Point out that the rules for the signs of quotients are the same as the rules for the signs of products.

Divide Integers

When you divide two integers with the **same sign**, the quotient is **positive**.	$(+) \div (+) = (+)$
	$(-) \div (-) = (+)$
When you divide two integers with **different signs**, the quotient is **negative**.	$(+) \div (-) = (-)$
	$(-) \div (+) = (-)$

Example 1 Same sign

Divide $(-36) \div (-4)$.

STEP 1 First determine the sign of the quotient.
$$(-) \div (-) = (+)$$
The signs are the same, so the quotient will be positive.

STEP 2 Divide as you would with whole numbers.
$$36 \div 4 = 9$$

So, $(-36) \div (-4) = 9$.

Example 2 Different signs

Divide $40 \div (-5)$.

STEP 1 First determine the sign of the quotient.
$$(+) \div (-) = (-)$$
The signs are different, so the quotient will be negative.

STEP 2 Divide as you would with whole numbers.
$$40 \div 5 = 8$$

So, $40 \div (-5) = -8$.

✔ Quick Check
Evaluate.

1 $21 \div (-7)$ _____

2 $(-48) \div (-6)$ _____

3 $(-49) \div 7$ _____

Practice on Your Own
Evaluate.

4 $(-12) \div (-6)$ _____

5 $54 \div (-9)$ _____

6 $(-35) \div (-7)$ _____

7 $12 \div (-1)$ _____

8 $72 \div 8$ _____

9 $(-18) \div 9$ _____

10 $(-15) \div 5$ _____

11 $56 \div (-8)$ _____

12 $(-16) \div (-16)$ _____

13 $64 \div (-8) \div (-2)$ _____

14 $(-81) \div (-9) \div (-3)$ _____

15 $(-100) \div 5 \div (-4)$ _____

Multiply Decimals by Positive Powers of 10

TEACHING STRATEGY

1. **Vocabulary** Make sure students understand the phrase *power of 10*. Remind them that a base of 10 with an exponent is called a power of 10. Explain that in a power of 10, the exponent tells how many times to use the base 10 as a factor.

2. **Teach** Direct students to Example 1. **Ask** By what power of 10 is the decimal being multiplied? [10^2] What is the value of 10^2? [100] To multiply a decimal by 100, how many places to the right do you move the decimal point? [2 places to the right] Direct students to Example 2. **Ask** By what power of 10 is the decimal being multiplied? [10^3] What is the value of 10^3? [1,000] To multiply a decimal by 1,000, how many places to the right do you move the decimal point? [3 places to the right] Are there enough digits to move the decimal point 3 places to the right? [No.] Tell students they must write 0 as a placeholder before they can write the decimal point.

3. **Quick Check** Look for these common errors.
   - Moving the decimal point to the left instead of the right.
   - Moving the decimal point an incorrect number of places.
   - Neglecting to insert one or more zeros that are needed as placeholders.

4. **Next Steps** Assign the practice exercises. For students who need more support, use the alternate teaching strategy.

Additional Teaching Resource
Online Transition Guide with Reteach and Extra Practice worksheets from previous grade levels

ALTERNATE INTERVENTION STRATEGY

Materials: TRT2 (Number Cards) plus additional cards featuring decimal points

Strategy: Use number cards to explore how to multiply a decimal by a power of 10.

1. Write the problem $4.38 \cdot 10^2$ on the board. Have students model the decimal number 4.38 with the number cards.

| 4 | · | 3 | 8 |

2. **Ask** To multiply 4.38 by 10^2, how many places should you move the decimal point? [2] In which direction will you move it? [to the right] Have students move the card with the decimal point two places to the right

| 4 | 3 | 8 | · |

On the board, write $4.38 \cdot 10^2 = 438$.

3. Write the problem $6.5 \cdot 10^3$ on the board. Have students model the decimal number 6.5 with the number cards.

| 6 | · | 5 |

4. **Ask** To multiply $6.5 \cdot 10^3$, how many places should you move the decimal point? [3] In which direction will you move it? [to the right] Can you move the decimal point 3 places to the right? [No.] Have students place two zero cards to the right of 5 so that they can move the decimal point 3 places to the right.

| 6 | 5 | 0 | 0 | · |

On the board, write $6.5 \cdot 10^3 = 6,500$.

Name _____ Date _____

Multiply Decimals by Positive Powers of 10

When you multiply a decimal by a positive power of 10, the decimal point moves to the right.

Example 1

$2.35 \cdot 10^2 = 2.\,3\,\,5$

Multiplying by 10^2 is the same as multiplying by 100. There are 2 zeros in 100, so move the decimal point 2 places to the right.

$2.35 \cdot 10^2 = 235$

Example 2

$2.35 \cdot 10^3 = 2.\,3\,\,5\,\,0$

Multiplying by 10^3 is the same as multiplying by 1,000. There are 3 zeros in 1,000, so move the decimal point 3 places to the right. Write 0 as a placeholder.

$2.35 \cdot 10^3 = 2,350$

✔ Quick Check
Evaluate.

1 $8.29 \cdot 10$

2 $0.76 \cdot 10^2$

3 $1.52 \cdot 10^3$

_____

_____

_____

Practice on Your Own
Evaluate.

4 $12.8 \cdot 10$

5 $4.91 \cdot 10^2$

6 $0.154 \cdot 10^3$

_____

_____

_____

7 $5.6 \cdot 10^2$

8 $0.64 \cdot 10$

9 $37.9 \cdot 10^2$

_____

_____

_____

10 $0.86 \cdot 10$

11 $0.207 \cdot 10^2$

12 $9.5 \cdot 10^4$

_____

_____

_____

13 $5.1 \cdot 10^3$

14 $2.86 \cdot 10$

15 $0.108 \cdot 10^4$

_____

_____

_____

Divide Decimals by Positive Powers of 10

NS SKILL 9

TEACHING STRATEGY

1. **Vocabulary** Make sure students understand the phrase *power of 10*. Remind them that a base of 10 with an exponent is called a power of 10. Explain that in a power of 10, the exponent tells how many times to use the base 10 as a factor.

2. **Teach** Direct students to Example 1. **Ask** By what power of 10 is the number being divided? [10^2] What is the value of 10^2? [100] To divide a number by 100, how many places to the left do you move the decimal point? [2 places to the left] Write a 0 to the left of the decimal point. Direct students to Example 2. **Ask** By what power of 10 is the number being divided? [10^3] What is the value of 10^3? [1,000] To divide a number by 1,000, how many places to the left do you move the decimal point? [3 places to the left] Are there enough digits to move the decimal point 3 places to the left? [No.] Write 0 as a placeholder between the decimal point and 6, and write another 0 to the left of the decimal point.

3. **Quick Check** Look for these common errors.
   • Moving the decimal point to the right instead of the left.
   • Moving the decimal point an incorrect number of places.
   • Neglecting to insert one or more zeros that are needed as placeholders.

4. **Next Steps** Assign the practice exercises. For students who need more support, use the alternate teaching strategy.

Additional Teaching Resource

🖰 Online Transition Guide with Reteach and Extra Practice worksheets from previous grade levels

ALTERNATE INTERVENTION STRATEGY

Materials: TRT2 (Number Cards) plus additional cards featuring decimal points

Strategy: Use number cards to explore how to divide a decimal by a power of 10.

1. Write the problem $13.7 \div 10^2$ on the board. Use number cards to model 13.7.

   $\boxed{1}$ $\boxed{3}$ $\boxed{\cdot}$ $\boxed{7}$

2. **Ask** To divide 13.7 by 10^2, how many places should you move the decimal point? [2] In which direction will you move it? [to the left] Have students move the card with the decimal point two places to the left. Point out that they should place a zero card to the left of the decimal point.

   $\boxed{0}$ $\boxed{\cdot}$ $\boxed{1}$ $\boxed{3}$ $\boxed{7}$

   On the board, write $13.7 \div 10^2 = 0.137$.

3. Write the problem $85.2 \div 10^3$ on the board. Use number cards to model 85.2.

   $\boxed{8}$ $\boxed{5}$ $\boxed{\cdot}$ $\boxed{2}$

4. **Ask** To divide 85.2 by 10^3, how many places should you move the decimal point? [3] In which direction will you move it? [to the left] Can you move the decimal point 3 places to the left? [No.] Have students place one zero card to the left of 8 and then move the decimal point 3 places to the left. Remind them also to place a zero card to the left of the decimal point.

   $\boxed{0}$ $\boxed{\cdot}$ $\boxed{0}$ $\boxed{8}$ $\boxed{5}$ $\boxed{2}$

   On the board, write $85.2 \div 10^3 = 0.0852$.

Divide Decimals by Positive Powers of 10

When you divide a decimal by a positive power of 10, the decimal point moves to the left.

Example 1

$68 \div 10^2 = 0\ 6\ 8$

Dividing by 10^2 is the same as dividing by 100. There are 2 zeros in 100, so move the decimal point 2 places to the left. Then write a 0 to the left of the decimal point.

$68 \div 10^2 = 0.68$

Example 2

$68 \div 10^3 = 0\ 0\ 6\ 8.$

Dividing by 10^3 is the same as dividing by 1,000. There are 3 zeros in 1,000, so move the decimal point 3 places to the left. Write 0 as a placeholder between the decimal point and 6. Finally, write a 0 to the left of the decimal point.

$68 \div 10^3 = 0.068$

✔ Quick Check
Evaluate.

1 $29 \div 10$

2 $6.3 \div 10^2$

3 $521 \div 10^3$

_____

_____

_____

Practice on Your Own
Evaluate.

4 $72.8 \div 10$

5 $32.1 \div 10^2$

6 $496 \div 10^2$

_____

_____

_____

7 $3 \div 10$

8 $84 \div 10^2$

9 $739 \div 10$

_____

_____

_____

10 $16 \div 10$

11 $305 \div 10^2$

12 $156 \div 10^3$

_____

_____

_____

13 $53.1 \div 10^3$

14 $9.86 \div 10^2$

15 $20.8 \div 10^3$

_____

_____

_____

Identify Equivalent Equations

TEACHING STRATEGY

1. **Vocabulary** Make sure students understand the term *equivalent equations*. Remind them that two equations are equivalent if they have the same solution.

2. **Teach** Direct students to Step 1 of Example 1. **Ask** How can you check that 10 is a solution of $x - 3 = 7$? [Substitute 10 for x in the equation.] Direct students to Step 2 of Example 1. **Ask** How can you check that 10 is a solution of $2x = 20$? [Substitute 10 for x in the equation.] Point out to students that when the solutions are the same, the equations are equivalent. Direct students to Step 1 of Example 2. **Ask** Why do you subtract 5 from both sides first? [You need to isolate the variable.] Direct students to Step 2 of Example 2. **Ask** Why do you multiply both sides of the equation by 3? [Because 3 times $\frac{1}{3}$ equals 1, so you have $1x$, or just x.] Point out to students that when the solutions are different, the equations are not equivalent.

3. **Quick Check** Look for these common errors.
   - Performing an operation on only one side of an equation, resulting in an incorrect solution.
   - Forgetting to check that the solution to an equation is correct.

4. **Next Steps** Assign the practice exercises. For students who need more support, use the alternate teaching strategy.

Additional Teaching Resource

 Online Transition Guide with Reteach and Extra Practice worksheets from previous grade levels

ALTERNATE INTERVENTION STRATEGY

Materials: TRT49 (Equivalent Equation Match Cards)

Strategy: Have students play a matching game to practice identifying equivalent equations.

1. Assign or have students select partners. Distribute one deck of cards to each pair.

2. Tell students to shuffle the cards and arrange them face down on their desks in a 3-by-4 grid.

3. Have students take turns turning over two of the upside-down cards. The student should study the equations featured on the card and say whether or not the equations are equivalent. (Tell students they may use pencil and paper to solve the equations.)

4. If the equations are not equivalent, the student flips the cards back over, and play passes to the partner. If the equations are equivalent, the student keeps the pair of cards and takes another turn.

5. Point out to students that, even when it is not their turn, they still should be solving the equations, in order to help them later locate pairs of cards with equivalent equations. Tell students they may not note on their paper the location of cards with particular solutions. Remembering the location of specific cards must be done in their heads.

6. Play continues until all the pairs of equivalent equations have been found. At the end of the game, the student with the most cards is the winner.

Identify Equivalent Equations

Example 1

Determine whether the two given equations are equivalent equations.

$$x - 3 = 7 \text{ and } 2x = 20$$

STEP 1 Solve the first equation for x.

$$x - 3 = 7$$
$$x - 3 + 3 = 7 + 3 \quad \text{Add 3 to both sides.}$$
$$x = 10$$

STEP 2 Solve the second equation for x.

$$2x = 20$$
$$\frac{2x}{2} = \frac{20}{2} \quad \text{Divide both sides by 2.}$$
$$x = 10$$

STEP 3 Compare solutions, $x = 10$ and $x = 10$. The solutions are the same.

So, $x - 3 = 7$ and $2x = 20$ are equivalent equations.

Example 2

Determine whether the two given equations are equivalent equations.

$$3x + 5 = 26 \text{ and } \frac{1}{3}x = 21$$

STEP 1 Solve the first equation for x.

$$3x + 5 = 26$$
$$3x + 5 - 5 = 26 - 5 \quad \text{Subtract 5 from both sides.}$$
$$3x = 21$$
$$\frac{3x}{3} = \frac{21}{3} \quad \text{Divide both sides by 3.}$$
$$x = 7$$

STEP 2 Solve the second equation for x.

$$3\left(\frac{1}{3}x\right) = 3(21) \quad \text{Multiply both sides by 3.}$$
$$x = 63$$

STEP 3 Compare solutions, $x = 7$ and $x = 63$. The solutions are not the same.

So, $3x + 5 = 26$ and $\frac{1}{3}x = 21$ are not equivalent equations.

✔ Quick Check

On a separate sheet of paper, tell whether each pair of equations is equivalent or not equivalent. Explain.

1 $x + 19 = 26$ and $x = 7$

2 $4(x + 1) = 20$ and $6x = 12$

3 $0.5x + 2 = 2.5x$ and $x = 1$

4 $\frac{1}{4}x = 8$ and $2x - 15 = 17$

Practice on Your Own
On a separate sheet of paper, tell whether each pair of equations is equivalent or not equivalent. Explain.

5 $4x = 56$ and $\frac{1}{6}x = 3$

6 $5x - 3 = 27$ and $4(x - 5) = 4$

7 $3.2x = 1.2x + 12$ and $x = 12$

8 $2(x + 7) = 10$ and $3(x - 1) = -9$

Write a Linear Equation to Relate Two Quantities

TEACHING STRATEGY

1. **Vocabulary** Make sure students understand the term *linear equation*. Remind them that a linear equation may have one or two variables.

2. **Teach** Point out to students that an algebraic equation is a mathematical way of writing a sentence. Tell students that associating key words with the correct operation is critical to being able to make the connection between words and algebra. Direct students to Example 1. **Ask** If Mindy's age is 3 years more than Evan's age, how do you find Mindy's age? [Add 3 to Evan's age.] **Ask** Whose age is Mindy's age dependent on? [Evan's age]. Direct students to Example 2. **Ask** If each box of crayons contains 12 crayons, how can you find the total number of crayons in *n* boxes? [Multiply 12 times the number of boxes of crayons.] **Ask** What is the total number of crayons dependent on? [the number of boxes of crayons bought] Point out to students that the dependent variable is usually alone on one side of the equation.

3. **Quick Check** Look for these common errors.
   - Using the wrong operation due to confusion about the meaning of key words in the description of the situation.
   - Misidentifying the dependent and independent variables.

4. **Next Steps** Assign the practice exercises. For students who need more support, use the alternate teaching strategy.

Additional Teaching Resource
🖱 Online Transition Guide with Reteach and Extra Practice worksheets from previous grade levels

ALTERNATE INTERVENTION STRATEGY

Materials: none

Strategy: Use input/output tables to write a linear equation.

1. Draw the following input/output table on the board.

Time, (t hours)	2	3	4
Distance, (d miles)	100	150	200

2. Tell students that the table shows data about the time traveled and distance covered for a car driven on a highway. **Ask** What is the relationship between time and distance? [The distance is 50 times the number of hours.] **Ask** What equation can you write that shows this? [$d = 50t$] What does the distance depend on? [the time] Which is the dependent variable? [d] What is the independent variable? [t]

3. Draw the following tables on the board. For each table, have students write an equation and identify the dependent and independent variables. (Possible answers shown. Answers for dependent variable and independent variable will vary, depending on the equations students write.)

Gallons, g	2	3	4
Distance, d	8	12	16

[$d = 4g$; Independent: g, Dependent: d.
OR $g = \frac{1}{4}d$; Independent: d, Dependent: g]

Hours, h	2	3	8
Earnings, e	20	30	80

[$e = 10h$; Independent: h, Independent: e]

Kim's age, k	6	9	13
Sam's age, s	8	11	15

[$s = k + 2$; Independent: k, Dependent: s.
OR $k = s - 2$; Independent: s, Dependent: k]

Write a Linear Equation to Relate Two Quantities

Example 1

Mindy is 3 years older than Evan. Express Mindy's age, m, in terms of Evan's age, e.

$$m = e + 3$$

When the equation is written this way, Mindy's age, m, depends on Evan's age, e. So the dependent variable is m, and the independent variable is e.

Example 2

Crayons are packed 12 to a box. Find the total number of crayons, t, in n boxes of crayons.

$$t = 12n$$

The total number of crayons, t, depends on the number of boxes of crayons bought, n. So the dependent variable is t, and the independent variable is n.

✔ Quick Check

Write a linear equation for each situation. Identify the independent and dependent variables.

1 Ana is making bouquets. Each bouquet includes 4 more roses, r, than carnations, c. Express the number of roses, r, in terms of the number of carnations, c.

_____

2 Jordan gets $5 for each newspaper subscription that he sells. Find the total amount, t, Jordan will receive for selling s subscriptions.

_____

Practice on Your Own
Write a linear equation for each situation. Identify the independent and dependent variables.

3 Kristi earns $1 more per hour than Mario. Express the amount that Kristi earns, k, in terms of the amount that Mario earns, m.

_____

4 Isaac earns $9 per hour. Find the total amount, t, Isaac earns if he works for h hours.

_____

5 The length of a desk is three times its width, w. Express the perimeter, P, of the desk in terms of the width.

_____

Solve Algebraic Equations

TEACHING STRATEGY

1. **Vocabulary** Make sure students understand the terms *algebraic equation* and *variable*. Remind them that to solve an algebraic equation, you need to isolate the variable on one side of the equals sign.

2. **Teach** Review the order of operations: multiply, divide, add, and subtract in order from left to right. Tell students to follow the order of operations in reverse as they select operations to use to solve a multi-step equation. Encourage students to move the smaller variable expression, rather than the larger one, to avoid having a negative coefficient. Direct students to Example 1. **Ask** On which side do you want to isolate the variable, and why? [On the left side so the coefficient of the variable will be positive.] Direct students to Example 2. Point out that you need to use the Distributive Property before you use inverse operations.

3. **Quick Check** Look for these common errors.
   - Performing an operation on only one side of an equation, producing an equation that is not equivalent.
   - Forgetting to distribute a factor across all the terms inside parentheses, producing an equation that is not equivalent.

4. **Next Steps** Assign the practice exercises. For students who need more support, use the alternate teaching strategy.

Additional Teaching Resource
Online Transition Guide with Reteach and Extra Practice worksheets from previous grade levels

ALTERNATE INTERVENTION STRATEGY

Materials: none

Strategy: Solve algebraic equations to complete a magic square.

1. Explain that a magic square is a square in which all the rows, columns, and diagonals have the same sum. Give the following example.

2	7	6
9	5	1
4	3	8

2. Tell students that they are going to complete another magic square by solving equations. Have students draw the following magic square on a piece of paper.

a.	b.	c.
d.	0	e.
−1	f.	3

3. Instruct students to solve each of the equations below and write the answer in the corresponding box. When complete, the students should confirm that they have created a magic square.

   a. $4x + 5 = 6x + 11$
   b. $10x - 3 = 15 + x$
   c. $5(x + 1) = 2(3x + 2)$
   d. $\frac{1}{2}x + 6 = 2x$
   e. $2(x - 5) = 3x + 3(x + 2)$
   f. $5(x - 3) = 3x - 19$

   [Answers: a. −3; b. 2; c. 1; d. 4; e. −4; f. −2]

Solve Algebraic Equations

Example 1 Variable on both sides of the equation

Get the variable terms on one side of the equation and the number terms on the other side.

$15x - 4 = 12x + 5$	
$15x - 12x - 4 = 12x - 12x + 5$	Subtract 12x from both sides.
$3x - 4 = 5$	Simplify.
$3x - 4 + 4 = 5 + 4$	Add 4 to both sides.
$3x = 9$	Simplify.
$\dfrac{3x}{3} = \dfrac{9}{3}$	Divide both sides by 3.
$x = 3$	Simplify.

Example 2 Distributive property

To remove parentheses, apply the distributive property.

$5(2x + 3) - 3x = 29$	
$10x + 15 - 3x = 29$	Use the distributive property.
$7x + 15 = 29$	Combine like terms.
$7x + 15 - 15 = 29 - 15$	Subtract 15 from both sides.
$7x = 14$	Simplify.
$\dfrac{7x}{7} = \dfrac{14}{7}$	Divide both sides by 7.
$x = 2$	Simplify.

✔ Quick Check
Solve each equation.

1 $9p = 2p + 63$ _____

2 $\frac{2}{3}b = 10 - \frac{1}{6}b$ _____

3 $8a + 2(3a - 1) = 26$ _____

4 $4(5y + 4) = 9(y - 8)$ _____

Practice on Your Own
Solve each equation.

5 $7k + 18 = 3k - 58$ _____

6 $\frac{3}{4}x = 4 + \frac{1}{3}x$ _____

7 $2(4z - 5) - 6z = 36$ _____

8 $3(2r - 1) = 9(2r - 5)$ _____

9 $3(3 - c) + 8c = 27 - 4c$ _____

10 $11d + 3(d - 7) = 4(7 - 2d) + 17$ _____

Represent Fractions as Repeating Decimals

TEACHING STRATEGY

1. **Vocabulary** Make sure students understand the term *repeating decimal*. Remind them that in a repeating decimal there can be one digit that repeats or a group of digits that repeats, and that the digits that repeat can start right after the decimal point or at a digit further from the decimal point.

2. **Teach** Work through Steps 1 and 2 of Example 1. Direct students to Step 3 of Example 1. Explain that you keep dividing until you notice that the remainders in the division start repeating. **Ask** What remainder starts to repeat? [4] What digit repeats in the quotient? [6] Tell students to write the decimal 0.16 and put a bar only over the 6 to represent 0.166…. Work through Steps 1 and 2 of Example 2. Direct students to Step 3 of Example 2. **Ask** What remainders start to repeat? [4 and 7] What digits repeat in the quotient? [63] Tell students to write the decimal 0.63 and put a bar over 63 to represent 0.6363…

3. **Quick Check** Look for these common errors.
   - Incorrectly dividing the denominator by the numerator instead of the numerator by the denominator to find the decimal.
   - Incorrectly drawing a bar over digits that do not repeat.

4. **Next Steps** Assign the practice exercises. For students who need more support, use the alternate teaching strategy.

Additional Teaching Resource

 Online Transition Guide with Reteach and Extra Practice worksheets from previous grade levels

ALTERNATE INTERVENTION STRATEGY

Materials: TRT50 (Repeating Fraction Cards)

Strategy: Have students play a matching game to practice representing fractions as repeating decimals.

1. Distribute one set of fraction cards and one set of repeating decimal cards to each student.

2. Tell students to spread the cards out face up on their desk.

3. One at a time, have students compute the repeating decimal for each fraction card. Remind them to:
   - Divide the numerator by the denominator.
   - First write a decimal point and several zeros at the end of the dividend.
   - Divide until the remainder starts repeating.
   - Draw a bar over the digits in the quotient that repeat.

4. For each repeating fraction for which they calculate a repeating decimal, students should locate the corresponding decimal card. Point out that there are extra repeating decimal cards, so not all the decimal cards will be used. [Answers: $\frac{4}{37} = 0.\overline{108}$; $\frac{17}{18} = 0.9\overline{4}$; $\frac{80}{99} = 0.\overline{80}$; $\frac{97}{99} = 0.\overline{97}$; $\frac{9}{11} = 0.\overline{81}$; $\frac{35}{36} = 0.97\overline{2}$]

Represent Fractions as Repeating Decimals

Example 1	One digit repeats

Write $\frac{1}{6}$ as a decimal. Use bar notation.

STEP 1 Divide the numerator by the denominator.

$$\frac{1}{6} \rightarrow 6\overline{)1}$$

STEP 2 At the end of the dividend, write a decimal point followed by zeros. Place a decimal point directly above the one in the dividend.

$$6\overline{)1.000}$$

STEP 3 Divide as you would with whole numbers until the remainders start repeating.

```
   0.166
6)1.000
 - 6
   40
 - 36
   40
 - 36
    4
```

STEP 4 The digit 6 repeats, so draw a bar over the 6.

$\frac{1}{6} = 0.1\overline{6}$

Example 2	A group of digits repeat

Write $\frac{7}{11}$ as a decimal. Use bar notation.

STEP 1 Divide the numerator by the denominator.

$$\frac{7}{11} \rightarrow 11\overline{)7}$$

STEP 2 At the end of the dividend, write a decimal point followed by zeros. Place a decimal point directly above the one in the dividend.

$$7\overline{)11.0000}$$

STEP 3 Divide as you would with whole numbers until the remainders start repeating.

```
    0.6363
11)7.0000
 - 66
   40
 - 33
   70
 - 66
   40
 - 33
    7
```

STEP 4 The group of digits, 63, repeats, so draw a bar over the 63.

$\frac{7}{11} = 0.\overline{63}$

✔ Quick Check

Write the decimal for each fraction. Use bar notation.

1 $\frac{2}{9}$ _____

2 $\frac{4}{11}$ _____

3 $\frac{19}{12}$ _____

Practice on Your Own

Write the decimal for each fraction. Use bar notation.

4 $\frac{13}{18}$ _____

5 $\frac{47}{99}$ _____

6 $\frac{25}{66}$ _____

7 $\frac{6}{7}$ _____

8 $\frac{17}{24}$ _____

9 $\frac{37}{33}$ _____

Recognize Direct Proportion in Graphs

TEACHING STRATEGY

1. **Vocabulary** Make sure students understand the terms *origin* and *direct proportion*. Ask a volunteer to name the coordinates of the origin, (0, 0). Remind students that two quantities, x and y, are in direct proportion if $\frac{y}{x} = k$ or $y = kx$, where k is a constant value. Point out that this means the ratio $\frac{y}{x}$ is the same for all ordered pairs (x, y).

2. **Teach** Review the three conditions that a graph must meet in order to be a graph of a direct proportion, as listed at the top of the page. Direct students to Example 1. **Ask** Is the graph a straight line? [Yes.] Does the line pass through the origin? [Yes.] Does the line lie on either of the axes? [No.] So, does this graph represent a direct proportion? [Yes.] Direct students to Example 2. **Ask** Is the graph a straight line? [Yes.] Does the line pass through the origin? [No.] Does this graph represent a direct proportion? [No.]

3. **Quick Check** Look for these common errors.
   • Incorrectly identifying a graph as showing a direct proportion if it passes through the origin, even if the graph is not a straight line.
   • Incorrectly identifying a graph as showing a direct proportion if it is a straight line, even though it does not pass through the origin.

4. **Next Steps** Assign the practice exercises. For students who need more support, use the alternate teaching strategy.

Additional Teaching Resource

🖱 Online Transition Guide with Reteach and Extra Practice worksheets from previous grade levels

ALTERNATE INTERVENTION STRATEGY

Materials: TRT51A, TRT51B (Graph Cards)

Strategy: Have students practice recognizing graphs of direct proportion by playing a card game.

1. Assign or have students select partners. Distribute one deck of cards to each pair.

2. Write the following statement on the board.

   A graph represents a direct proportion only if it satisfies all three of the following requirements.
   a. It is a straight line.
   b. It passes through the origin, (0, 0).
   c. It does not lie along the x-axis or the y-axis.

3. Have students take turns choosing cards from the deck. The student should study the graph featured on the card and say whether the graph does or does not represent a direct proportion. If the student is correct, he or she is awarded a point.

4. If the graph does not represent a direct proportion, the student must also identify at least one reason why it does not. The student is awarded one point for each correct reason identified.

5. Remind students that they can refer to the list of statements on the board for help. Tell them that in the event of a disagreement over a graph, they should raise their hands and you will identify the correct answer.

6. Play continues until all the graph cards have been identified. The student with the most points is the winner.

RP
SKILL 14 # Recognize Direct Proportion in Graphs

The graph of a direct proportion must:
- be a straight line,   • pass through the origin (0, 0),   • not lie along the x-axis or y-axis.

Example 1

Tell whether the graph represents a direct proportion. Explain.

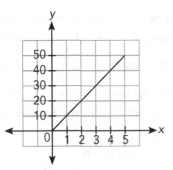

Yes. The graph is a straight line passing through (0, 0), so it represents a direct proportion.

Example 2

Tell whether the graph represents a direct proportion. Explain.

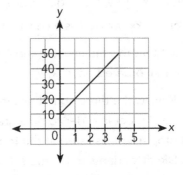

No. Although it is a straight line, the graph does not pass through (0, 0), so it does not represent a direct proportion.

✓ Quick Check
Tell whether the graph represents a direct proportion.

1
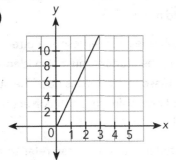

2
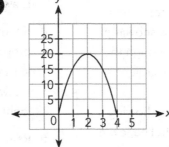

3
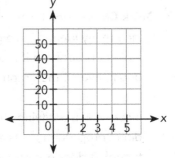

Practice on Your Own
Tell whether the graph represents a direct proportion.

4
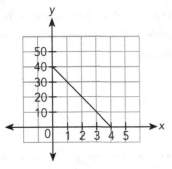

5
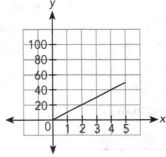

6
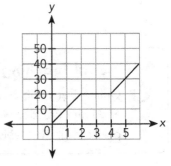

Graph Linear Equations Using a Table of Values

EE SKILL 15

TEACHING STRATEGY

1. **Vocabulary** Make sure students understand the term *ordered pair*. Remind them that each ordered pair is a set of *x* and *y* values that make the equation true. An ordered pair can be plotted on a coordinate grid with an *x*-axis and a *y*-axis. **Ask** Which axis is the horizontal axis? [the *x*-axis]

2. **Teach** Direct students to Step 1. **Ask** Does it matter what values you choose for *x*? [No.] Note that any number will work, but smaller numbers are easier to work with and graph. Direct students to Step 2. **Ask** Which value comes first in an ordered pair? [*x*] How do you plot an ordered pair? [Start at (0, 0). The *x* value indicates how many units to move left or right, and the *y* value indicates how many units to move up or down.] Direct students to Step 3. **Ask** Why does the line extend past the plotted points? [The line represents all ordered pairs that are solutions to the equation, not just the individual points that were plotted to locate the line.]

3. **Quick Check** Look for these common errors.
   • Plotting points that do not form a straight line due to mathematical errors made when finding *y* values.
   • Reversing the *x*- and *y*-coordinates when plotting points.

4. **Next Steps** Assign the practice exercises. For students who need more support, use the alternate teaching strategy.

Additional Teaching Resource

 Online Transition Guide with Reteach and Extra Practice worksheets from previous grade levels

ALTERNATE INTERVENTION STRATEGY

Materials: TRT8 (Graph Paper), ruler

Strategy: Use *x*- and *y*-intercepts to graph linear equations.

1. Distribute graph paper and rulers. Have students draw and label an *x*-axis and a *y*-axis on the graph paper. Write the equation $x + y = 1$ on the board.

2. **Ask** How many points determine a line? [2] Point out that the graph of a linear equation can be drawn by plotting only the points at which the line crosses the *x*-axis and *y*-axis.

3. **Ask** When a graph crosses the *y*-axis, what is the value of *x*? [0] Explain that the point at which a graph crosses the *y*-axis is called the *y*-intercept. To find the *y*-intercept, students can substitute 0 for *x* in the equation and solve for *y*. **Ask** What is the value of *y* when *x* = 0? [1] What is the ordered pair for *x* = 0 and *y* = 1? [(0, 1)] Where is that point located? [where the vertical line through 0 on the *x*-axis meets the horizontal line through 1 on the *y*-axis] Have students plot this point.

4. **Ask** When a graph crosses the *x*-axis, what is the value of *y*? [0] Explain that the point at which a graph crosses the *x*-axis is called the *x*-intercept. To find the *x*-intercept, students can substitute 0 for *y* in the equation and solve for *x*. **Ask** What is the value of *x* when *y* = 0? [1] What is the ordered pair for *x* = 1 and *y* = 0? [(1, 0)] Have students plot this point.

5. Now students can draw a line through the two points to graph the equation.

6. Repeat this activity several times with different linear equations, such as $x + 2y = 6$ and $x - y = 4$.

Graph Linear Equations Using a Table of Values

Example

Graph the equation $y = 3x - 3$.

STEP 1 Make a table of values. Substitute each x value into the equation to find the corresponding y value.

For example, substitute 0 for x.

$y = 3(0) - 3$

$y = -3$

x	0	1	2	3
y = 3x – 3	–3	0	3	6

STEP 2 Plot each ordered pair on the coordinate grid.

STEP 3 Draw a line through the points.

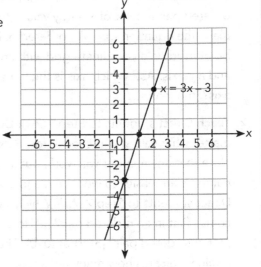

✔ Quick Check

Copy and complete the table of values for each linear equation. Then draw its graph on a coordinate grid.

1 $y = 2x$

x	0	1	2	3
y = 2x	?	?	?	?

2 $y = x - 2$

x	0	1	2	3
y = x – 2	?	?	?	?

Practice on Your Own

Copy and complete the table of values for each linear equation. Then draw its graph on a coordinate grid.

3 $y = -3x$

x	0	1	2	3
y = –3x	?	?	?	?

4 $y = -x + 1$

x	0	1	2	3
y = –x + 1	?	?	?	?

5 $y = -4x + 6$

x	0	1	2	3
y = –4x + 6	?	?	?	?

6 $y = 3x - 5$

x	0	1	2	3
y = 3x – 5	?	?	?	?

Solve Real-World Problems Algebraically

TEACHING STRATEGY

1. **Vocabulary** Make sure students understand the terms *equation* and *variable*. Remind students that a variable is used to represent an unknown quantity.

2. **Teach** Have students read the problem in the Example. Tell them they can write an equation to help them solve the problem, but first they must determine what quantity they need to find and assign a variable to represent it. **Ask** What do you need to find? [Maxie's weight] Direct students to Step 1. **Ask** Does the variable need to be the letter x? [No. You can use any letter for the variable.] Direct students to Step 2. Point out how the equation mirrors the verbal sentence. Direct students to Step 3, and work through the solution with them. Direct students to Step 4. **Ask** Why is it important to check the answer? [If the answer does not match the given values in the problem, you know that you have made a mistake.]

3. **Quick Check** Look for these common errors.
   - Assigning a variable to one quantity in the problem and then mistakenly using it to represent another quantity.
   - Setting up the equation incorrectly, which may indicate confusion over the relationship between quantities or perhaps an inability to recognize which operations key words indicate.
   - Performing an inverse operation on only one side of the equation.

4. **Next Steps** Assign the practice exercises. For students who need more support, use the alternate teaching strategy.

Additional Teaching Resource

Online Transition Guide with Reteach and Extra Practice worksheets from previous grade levels

ALTERNATE INTERVENTION STRATEGY

Materials: TRT2 (Number Cards); additional cards featuring +, −, ·, = and *n*; blank cards

Strategy: Use number cards to explore how to write and solve algebraic equations.

1. Write the following problem on the board. The sum of twice a number and 6 is 20. Have students model the problem with their cards. Tell them if they need a number they do not have, to write it on a blank card.

$$\boxed{2} \quad \boxed{\cdot} \quad \boxed{n} \quad \boxed{+} \quad \boxed{6} \quad \boxed{=} \quad \boxed{20}$$

2. **Ask** What is the inverse operation of addition? [subtraction] Tell students to subtract 6 from both sides of the equation and then model the new equation.

$$\boxed{2} \quad \boxed{\cdot} \quad \boxed{n} \quad \boxed{=} \quad \boxed{14}$$

Ask What is the inverse operation of multiplication? [division] Tell students to divide each side of the equation by 2 and model the new equation.

$$\boxed{n} \quad \boxed{=} \quad \boxed{7}$$

Ask What is the value of *n*? [7]

3. Have students substitute 7 into the problem. **Ask** Does the answer check? [Yes, twice 7 is 14, and the sum of 14 and 6 is 20.]

4. Have students model and identify the unknown value in the following problems.
   - Three less than 4 times a number is 17. [5]
   - The sum of a number and 5 more than the number is 11. [3]

   Then have students model and solve real-world problems using the number cards.

EE
SKILL 16

Solve Real-World Problems Algebraically

Example

Madeleine has two dogs, Sam and Maxie. Sam weighs 8 pounds more than Maxie. Together the dogs weigh 50 pounds. How much does Maxie weigh?

STEP 1 Use a variable to represent the weight of one of the dogs.
Let x represent Maxie's weight.
Sam weighs 8 pounds more than Maxie, so $x + 8$ represents Sam's weight.

STEP 2 Write an equation to represent the situation.

Maxie's weight + Sam's weight = 50 pounds
$$x \qquad + \quad x + 8 \qquad = 50$$

STEP 3 Solve the equation.

$x + x + 8 = 50$	
$2x + 8 = 50$	Combine like terms.
$2x = 42$	Subtract 8 from each side of the equation.
$x = 21$	Divide each side of the equation by 2.

STEP 4 Check your answer.
If Maxie's weight is 21 pounds, then Sam's weight is $21 + 8$, or 29 pounds.
Add: $21 + 29 = 50$. Together the dogs weigh 50 pounds; the answer checks.

Answer the question: Maxie weighs 21 pounds.

✔ Quick Check
Solve. Show your work.

1 Emma bought a DVD and a video game. The DVD cost $4 less than the video game. Together they cost $42. How much did the DVD cost? _____

2 Last week Kevin and Yun mowed lawns. Kevin earned $10 less than 3 times as much as Yun earned. If Kevin earned $71, how much did Yun earn? _____

Practice on Your Own
Solve. Show your work.

3 Paul is 6 years younger than his sister Tabitha. The sum of their ages is 24. How old is Paul? _____

4 Carmen's Canoes rents canoes for a $15 fee plus $8 per hour. Lisa and Faruq paid $47 to rent a canoe. For how many hours did they rent the canoe? _____

Write Algebraic Expressions to Represent Unknown Quantities

TEACHING STRATEGY

1. **Vocabulary** Make sure students understand the term *algebraic expression*. Remind them that to solve real-world problems they will need to translate words, or a verbal expression, into an algebraic expression. Explain that an algebraic expression contains one or more variables and may contain operation symbols.

2. **Teach** Direct students to the Example. **Ask** How can you find how much Jason earned if he washed a certain number of cars? [Multiply the number of cars by how much he charged per car.] Do you know how many cars Jason washed? [No.] Explain that the variable x is used to represent the number of cars Jason washed. Since Jason charged $7 per car, you would multiply x by 7. **Ask** What operation would you use to show that Jason also earned $25 in tips? [addition] Point out that in the expression $7x + 25$, there is no multiplication symbol between 7 and x because the expression $7x$ means to multiply x by 7.

3. **Quick Check** Look for these common errors.
   - Choosing incorrect operations when writing algebraic expressions.
   - Writing terms in the wrong order when using subtraction or division.

4. **Next Steps** Assign the practice exercises. For students who need more support, use the alternate teaching strategy.

Additional Teaching Resource

 Online Transition Guide with Reteach and Extra Practice worksheets from previous grade levels

ALTERNATE INTERVENTION STRATEGY

Materials: index cards

Strategy: Practice matching verbal descriptions to algebraic expressions.

1. Write on each index card an algebraic expression such as the following.

$$x + 2, \ y - 4, \ 3b, \ \frac{a}{5}$$

2. Divide students into groups of four. Give each group a packet of index cards with the algebraic expressions, as well as some blank index cards.

3. Have one student hold up an index card with an algebraic expression. Taking turns, each student in the group should then state a verbal phrase that corresponds to the algebraic expression. Encourage students to use as many different phrases as possible. For example, for $x + 2$, here are some possible expressions: "2 more than x," "x increased by 2," and "the sum of x and 2." Students should record each phrase on the back of the index card.

4. For each algebraic expression, have a member of each group come up with a corresponding real-world situation. For example, for $x + 2$, here is a possible real-world situation: "Jill has x apples. Sam has 2 more apples than Jill. How many apples does Sam have?" The answer to this question is, "Sam has $(x + 2)$ apples." Have each group share their real-world situations with the class.

5. Repeat the activity with more complex algebraic expressions such as the following.

$$5x + 4, \ \frac{c}{3} + 7, \ 10 - 2d, \ \frac{n}{2} - 1$$

EE
SKILL 17

Write Algebraic Expressions to Represent Unknown Quantities

Example

On Saturday Jason washed x cars at a rate of \$7 per car. He also earned \$25 in tips. Write an algebraic expression for the total amount of money Jason earned washing cars on Saturday.

Product of x and 7   plus   25

$7 \cdot x$ +   25   Translate by parts.

$7x + 25$ Combine.

Jason earned $(7x + 25)$ dollars washing cars on Saturday.

✔ Quick Check
Write an algebraic expression for each of the following.

1 Kayla bought b books. Each book cost \$8. She used a coupon to get \$5 off the total price. Write an algebraic expression for the amount of money Kayla spent.

_____

2 n pens were divided equally among 5 students. One student, Dwayne, then bought 3 more pens. Write an algebraic expression for the number of pens Dwayne has.

_____

Practice on Your Own
Write an algebraic expression for each of the following.

3 Madison bowled x games. Each game cost \$4, and she rented shoes for \$2. Write an algebraic expression for the total amount of money Madison spent.

_____

4 Akira bought 9 packs of trading cards. Each pack has y cards. He gave 6 cards to his brother. Write an algebraic expression for the number of cards Akira has left.

_____

5 Sixty granola bars were shared equally among w friends. One friend, Kayla, gave 8 bars to her sister. Write an algebraic expression for the number of bars Kayla has left.

_____

Evaluate Algebraic Expressions

TEACHING STRATEGY	ALTERNATE INTERVENTION STRATEGY

TEACHING STRATEGY

1. **Vocabulary** Make sure students understand the terms *variable*, *evaluate*, and *algebraic expression*. Remind them that when they evaluate an algebraic expression, they substitute the given numerical value for the variable.

2. **Teach** Review the order of operations. Direct students to Example 1. **Ask** What operations are in the expression $3n + 2$? [multiplication and addition] According to the order of operations, which operation must you do first in this problem? [multiplication] Direct students to Example 2. **Ask** What operations are in the expression $14 - \frac{x}{3}$? [subtraction and division] According to the order of operations, which operation must you do first in this problem? [division]

3. **Quick Check** Look for these common errors.
   - Arriving at an incorrect result due to not following the order of operations correcty.
   - Arriving at an incorrect result due to making sign errors.

4. **Next Steps** Assign the practice exercises. For students who need more support, use the alternate teaching strategy.

Additional Teaching Resource
Online Transition Guide with Reteach and Extra Practice worksheets from previous grade levels

ALTERNATE INTERVENTION STRATEGY

Materials: TRT3 (Blank Tables)

Strategy: Use tables to practice evaluating expressions.

1. Draw the table below on the board. Have students copy it.

Value	Substitution	Simplification
−2	6( ) + 3	___ + 3 = ___
−1	6( ) + 3	___ + 3 = ___
0	6( ) + 3	___ + 3 = ___
1	6( ) + 3	___ + 3 = ___
2	6( ) + 3	___ + 3 = ___

2. **Ask** Based on the center column, what expression are you evaluating? [Possible answer: $6n + 3$] For what values are you evaluating the expression? [−2, −1, 0 , 1, 2] Have students complete the table and check their answers. [By column: −2, −1, 0, 1, 2; −12, −6, 0, 6, 12; −9, −3, 3, 9, 15]

3. Draw the table below on the board. Have students copy it.

Value	Substitution	Simplification
−4	$\frac{(\ \ )}{2} - 5$	___ − 5 = ___
−2	$\frac{(\ \ )}{2} - 5$	___ − 5 = ___
0	$\frac{(\ \ )}{2} - 5$	___ − 5 = ___
2	$\frac{(\ \ )}{2} - 5$	___ − 5 = ___

4. Have students identify the expression and complete the table. [Possible answer: $\frac{x}{2} - 5$; By column: −4, −2, 0, 2; −2, −1, 0, 1; −7, −6, −5, −4]

Evaluate Algebraic Expressions

Example 1

Evaluate $3n + 2$ when $n = -5$.

$3n + 2 = 3(-5) + 2$ Substitute -5 for n.

$\quad\quad = -15 + 2$ Multiply.

$\quad\quad = -13$ Add.

So, $3n + 2 = -13$ when $n = -5$.

Example 2

Evaluate $14 - \dfrac{x}{3}$ when $x = 9$.

$14 - \dfrac{x}{3} = 14 - \dfrac{9}{3}$ Substitute 9 for x.

$\quad\quad = 14 - 3$ Divide.

$\quad\quad = 11$ Subtract.

So, $14 - \dfrac{x}{3} = 11$ when $x = 9$.

✔ Quick Check

Evaluate each expression for the given value of the variable.

1 $4y - 9$ when $y = 2$

_____

2 $3 + \dfrac{1}{2}b$ when $b = -7$

_____

3 $6 + 7m$ when $m = -4$

_____

4 $\dfrac{k}{5} - 3$ when $k = 20$

_____

Practice on Your Own
Evaluate each expression for the given value of the variable.

5 $15 - 4n$ when $n = 6$

_____

6 $13 + 4w$ when $w = -2$

_____

7 $-2y - 5$ when $y = -1$

_____

8 $10 + 6z$ when $z = -2$

_____

9 $15 - 5r$ when $r = 3$

_____

10 $\dfrac{h}{4} + 1$ when $h = 14$

_____

11 $8p + 5$ when $p = \dfrac{3}{4}$

_____

12 $3 + \dfrac{2}{3}w$ when $w = -9$

_____

Understand Squares and Square Roots

TEACHING STRATEGY

1. **Vocabulary** Make sure students understand the terms *base*, *exponent*, and *power*. Write 8^2 on the board. Explain that 8 is the base and 2 is the exponent, and the exponent tells how many times the base is used as a factor. Tell students that 8^2 is read as "8 squared" or "8 raised to the second power" or "the second power of 8."

2. **Teach** Remind students that they can find the squares of negative numbers, too. **Ask** When you square a number, how many times is that number used as a factor? [two times] How do you find the value of $(-5)^2$? [Multiply: $(-5) \cdot (-5)$.] What is the square of –5? [25] Direct students to Example 2. Point out that finding the square root of a number is the inverse, or opposite, of finding the square of a number. **Ask** How does knowing $(-5) \cdot (-5) = 25$ help you to find the square roots of 25? [The square root of a number is a number that, when multiplied by itself, equals the original number. Since both $(-5) \cdot (-5) = 25$ and $5 \cdot 5 = 25$, then the square roots of 25 are –5 and 5.]

3. **Quick Check** Look for these common errors.
   - When raising a number to the second power, doubling instead of squaring the number.
   - Multiplying a base by the exponent, instead of multiplying the base by itself.
   - Forgetting that a square has both a positive and a negative square root.

4. **Next Steps** Assign the practice exercises. For students who need more support, use the alternate teaching strategy.

Additional Teaching Resource

Online Transition Guide with Reteach and Extra Practice worksheets from previous grade levels

ALTERNATE INTERVENTION STRATEGY

Materials: TRT8 (Graph Paper)

Strategy: Use coordinate-grid models to find squares and square roots of numbers.

1. Explain to students that they can use grid paper to help determine the squares and square roots of numbers.

2. Have students form two squares by shading in 3 rows and 3 columns on the grid paper as shown. These are representations of 3^2 and $(-3)^2$, or the squares of three and negative three, because they form squares.

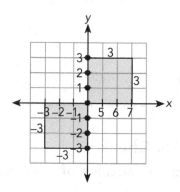

3. Have students count the number of shaded squares that make up each larger square. A total of 9 squares make up each larger square. **Ask** Instead of counting, how could you find the areas of the larger squares? [Multiply the length times the width: $3 \cdot 3 = 9$, and $(-3) \cdot (-3) = 9$.] Help students relate the areas to **the** values of the squares: $3^2 = 9$ and $(-3)^2 = 9$.

4. Explain to students that finding the square roots of a number is the opposite of finding the square of a number. **Ask** Can you form a large square using 25 small squares? [Yes.] How many small squares make up one side of the larger square? [5] What is the positive square root of 25? [5] What is the negative square root of 25? [–5]

5. Have students repeat this with 4 and –4.

Understand Squares and Square Roots

Squaring a number and finding the square root of a number are inverse operations.

$7^2 = 7 \cdot 7 = 49$, so the square of 7 is 49, and the positive square root of 49 is 7.

$(-7)^2 = (-7) \cdot (-7) = 49$, so the square of -7 is 49, and the negative square root of 49 is -7.

The radical symbol $\sqrt{}$ indicates the positive square root, so $\sqrt{49} = 7$.

Example 1 Squares

Find the square of $\frac{1}{6}$.

STEP 1 Write a multiplication expression using $\frac{1}{6}$ as a factor 2 times.

$$\frac{1}{6} \cdot \frac{1}{6}$$

STEP 2 Multiply to find the square.

$$\frac{1}{6} \cdot \frac{1}{6} = \frac{1}{36}$$

The square of $\frac{1}{6}$, written $\left(\frac{1}{6}\right)^2$, is $\frac{1}{36}$.

Example 2 Square Roots

Find the square roots of 81.

STEP 1 Think: What number times itself is equal to 81?

$$x \cdot x = 81$$

STEP 2 Use your knowledge of multiplication facts to find the positive square root.

$$9 \cdot 9 = 81$$

STEP 3 Find the negative square root.

$$(-9) \cdot (-9) = 81$$

The square roots of 81 are 9 and -9.

✔ Quick Check

Find the square of each number.

1 -4 _____

2 $\frac{1}{5}$ _____

3 $-\frac{1}{3}$ _____

Find the square roots of each number.

4 36 _____

5 $\frac{1}{16}$ _____

6 144 _____

Practice on Your Own
Find the square of each number.

7 8 _____

8 $\frac{1}{8}$ _____

9 -10 _____

Find the square roots of each number.

10 400 _____

11 9 _____

12 $\frac{1}{100}$ _____

Understand Cubes and Cube Roots

TEACHING STRATEGY

1. **Vocabulary** Make sure students understand the terms *base*, *cube*, *exponent*, and *power*. Write 4^3 on the board. Explain that 4 is the base and 3 is the exponent, and the exponent tells how many times the base is used as a factor. Note that 4^3 is read as "4 cubed" or "4 raised to the third power" or "the third power of 4."

2. **Teach** Explain to students that when they find the cube of a number, they will apply an exponent of 3. Stress that this is not the same as multiplying the number by 3. **Ask** When you cube a number, how many times is that number used as a factor? [three times] How do you find the value of 5^3? [Multiply: $5 \cdot 5 \cdot 5$.] What is the cube of 5? [125] Point out that finding the cube root of a number is the inverse, or opposite, of finding the cube of a number. **Ask** How does knowing $5 \cdot 5 \cdot 5 = 125$ help you to find the cube root of 125? [The cube root of a number is a number that, when multiplied three times, equals the original number. So the cube root of 125 is 5.] Have students read Example 2. Relate the two statements $10^3 = 1{,}000$ and $\sqrt[3]{1{,}000} = 10$.

3. **Quick Check** Look for these common errors.
   - When raising the number to the third power, tripling instead of cubing the number.
   - Multiplying a base by the exponent, instead of multiplying the base by itself.
   - Forgetting that the cube of a negative number is negative.

4. **Next Steps** Assign the practice exercises. For students who need more support, use the alternate teaching strategy.

Additional Teaching Resource
🖱 Online Transition Guide with Reteach and Extra Practice worksheets from previous grade levels

ALTERNATE INTERVENTION STRATEGY

Materials: TRT9 (Dot Paper)

Strategy: Use grid models to find cubes and cube roots of numbers.

1. Explain to students that they can use dot paper to help determine the cubes and cube roots of numbers.

2. Instruct students to sketch a cube on their dot paper as shown. Point out that this is a geometric representation of 5^3, or the cube of 5, because it forms a cube with edges that measure 5 units each.

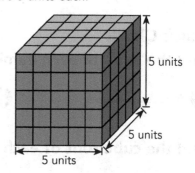

3. Have students count the number of cubes that make up the larger cube. There are a total of 125 cubes. **Ask** Instead of counting, how could you find the volume of the larger cube? [Multiply the length times the width times the height: $5 \cdot 5 \cdot 5 = 125$.] Help students relate the volume of 125 to the value of the cube: $5^3 = 125$.

4. Explain to students that finding the cube root of a number is the opposite of finding the cube of a number. **Ask** Can you form a large cube using 125 small cubes? [Yes.] How many small cubes make up one dimension of the larger cube? [5] Connect this to the fact that $\sqrt[3]{125} = 5$.

5. Have students repeat this exercise with 3 and with 6. **Ask** What is 3^3? [27] What is 6^3? [216] What is $\sqrt[3]{27}$? [3] What is $\sqrt[3]{216}$? [6]

EE
SKILL 20 # Understand Cubes and Cube Roots

Cubing a number and finding the cube root of a number are inverse operations.

$4^3 = 4 \cdot 4 \cdot 4 = 64$, so the cube of 4 is 64, and the cube root of 64 is 4.

Example 1

Find the cube of 5.

STEP 1 Write a multiplication expression using 5 as a factor 3 times.
$$5 \cdot 5 \cdot 5$$

STEP 2 Multiply to find the cube.
$$5 \cdot 5 \cdot 5 = 125$$

The cube of 5, written 5^3, is 125.

Example 2

Find the cube root of 1000.

STEP 1 Think: What number can I multiply three times to equal 1,000?
$$x \cdot x \cdot x = 1,000$$

STEP 2 Use your knowledge of multiplication facts to find the cube root.
$$10 \cdot 10 \cdot 10 = 1,000$$

The cube root of 1,000 written $\sqrt[3]{1,000}$, is 10.

✔ Quick Check
Find the cube of each number.

1 6 _____

2 –3 _____

3 8 _____

Find the cube root of each number.

4 8 _____

5 64 _____

6 729 _____

Practice on Your Own
Find the cube of each number.

7 4 _____

8 2 _____

9 –10 _____

10 1 _____

11 –11 _____

12 –5 _____

Find the cube root of each number.

13 343 _____

14 1 _____

15 27 _____

16 216 _____

17 512 _____

18 1,000,000 _____

19 The cube root of 1 is 1, but the cube root of 2 is not an integer. What is the next whole number, greater than 1, having a cube root that is a integer?

_____

Find Lengths of Horizontal and Vertical Line Segments in the Coordinate Plane

TEACHING STRATEGY

1. **Vocabulary** Make sure students understand the terms *horizontal* and *vertical*, and can identify the *x*-axis and *y*-axis.

2. **Teach** Work through Example 1 with students. Make sure students understand that they can move in either direction when counting the number of units between the endpoints since distance is always positive. Before beginning Example 2, have students identify the coordinates of all four endpoints. **Ask** What do you notice about the coordinates of points *A* and *B*? [They have the same *x*-coordinate, –3.] Explain that the endpoints of a vertical line segment will always have the same *x*-coordinate. **Ask** What do you notice about the coordinates of points *C* and *D*? [They have the same *y*-coordinate, –5.] Explain that the endpoints of a horizontal line segment will always have the same *y*-coordinate. Work through Example 2. **Ask** Why do we find the *absolute value* of the difference between the two coordinates? [because distance is always positive]

3. **Quick Check** Look for these common errors.
   - Mixing up *x*-coordinates and *y*-coordinates, indicating confusion about coordinate notation.
   - Computation errors when subtracting with negatives.

4. **Next Steps** Assign the practice exercises. For students who need more support, use the alternate teaching strategy.

Additional Teaching Resource

 Online Transition Guide with Reteach and Extra Practice worksheets from previous grade levels

ALTERNATE INTERVENTION STRATEGY

Materials: TRT5 (Coordinate Grids), colored pencils or markers

Strategy: Draw horizontal and vertical line segments on the coordinate plane and determine their lengths by counting units.

1. Tell students that they will draw vertical and horizontal segments on the coordinate plane and determine their lengths.

2. Instruct students to plot any point *A* in Quadrant I on a coordinate plane. Then have them plot a second point, *B*, in Quadrant 2 to form a horizontal line segment. **Ask** As you chose a location for point *B*, what did you know about its coordinates? [It must have the same *y*-coordinate as *A*.]

3. Have students use a colored pencil to draw a segment connecting *A* and *B*. **Ask** How can you find the length of segment *AB*? [Count the units between *A* and *B*.]

4. Have students choose a different colored pencil and repeat Step 2, this time drawing vertical segment *CD* with endpoints in Quadrant I and Quadrant IV. **Ask** As you chose a location for point *D*, what did you know about its coordinates? [It must have the same *x*-coordinate as *C*.]

5. Have students use a colored pencil to draw a segment connecting *C* and *D*. **Ask** How can you find the length of segment *CD*? [Count the units between *C* and *D*.]

6. Have students identify the coordinates of the endpoints of their line segments. Have them find the length of the segments again, this time by using absolute value. Guide them through the process as needed.

Find Lengths of Horizontal and Vertical Line Segments in the Coordinate Plane

Example 1 | Count Units

Find the lengths of $\overline{AB}$ and $\overline{CD}$.

For $\overline{AB}$: Count the number of units between A and B.
There are 4 units.

For $\overline{CD}$: Count the number of units between C and D.
There are 5 units.

$\overline{AB}$ is 4 units long. $\overline{CD}$ is 5 units long.

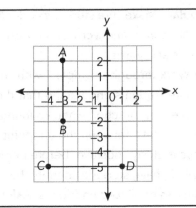

Example 2 | Use Absolute Value

Find the lengths of $\overline{AB}$ and $\overline{CD}$.

For $\overline{AB}$: A(–3, 2) and B(–3, –2) have the same x-coordinate.
Find the absolute value of the difference between their y-coordinates.
$$AB = |\,2 - (-2)\,| = |\,2 + 2\,| = |\,4\,| = 4$$

For $\overline{CD}$: C(–4, –5) and D(1, –5) have the same y-coordinate.
Find the absolute value of the difference between their x-coordinates.
$$CD = |\,-4 - 1\,| = |\,-5\,| = 5$$

$\overline{AB}$ is 4 units long. $\overline{CD}$ is 5 units long.

✔ Quick Check

Use graph paper to plot each pair of points in a coordinate plane. Connect the points to form a segment and find its length.

1 (–3, 5) and (4, 5) _____

2 (2, –4) and (2, 9) _____

Practice on Your Own

Use graph paper to plot each pair of points in a coordinate plane. Connect the points to form a segment and find its length.

3 (0, 9) and (0, –2) _____

4 (3, 5) and (–3, 5) _____

5 (7, –7) and (7, 0) _____

6 (–2, –4) and (–9, –4) _____

Find the Volume of Prisms and Pyramids

TEACHING STRATEGY

1. **Vocabulary** Make sure students understand the terms *prism*, *pyramid*, *base*, and *height*. Tell students that a prism has two bases, while a pyramid has only one base. Prisms and pyramids are named by the shape of their base(s). Explain that, although the worksheet shows only a triangular prism, the formula holds for all prisms. Similarly, although the worksheet shows only a rectangular pyramid, the formula holds for all pyramids.

2. **Teach** Have students first identify the bases and heights of these solids so that they can apply the formulas. **Ask** What units are used for the bases, and why? [square units, because you use the area of the base] How are the two formulas for volume the same, and how are they different? [Both formulas have *B* and *h* multiplied. The formula for volume of a pyramid also has a factor of $\frac{1}{3}$.] Direct students to the prism. **Ask** What shape are the bases? [triangles] What shape are the faces? [rectangles] How many faces are there? [3] Direct students to the pyramid. **Ask** What shape is the base? [rectangle] What shape are the faces, and how many are there? [4 triangles]

3. **Quick Check** Look for these common errors.
   • Confusing the formulas for the volume of a prism and the volume of a pyramid.
   • Using incorrect units in their answers, such as squared units.

4. **Next Steps** Assign the practice exercises to students who show understanding. For students who need more support, use the alternate teaching strategy.

Additional Teaching Resource
🖱 Online Transition Guide with Reteach and Extra Practice worksheets from previous grade levels

ALTERNATE INTERVENTION STRATEGY

Materials: none

Strategy: Have students find the volume of a rectangular prism.

1. On the board, draw the rectangular prism below.

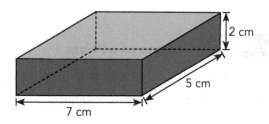

2. **Ask** What formula can we use to find the volume of a prism? [$V = Bh$] Write the formula on the board. **Ask** What kind of prism is this? [rectangular] So, what shape is its base? [a rectangle]

3. Tell students to assume that the bottom face of the prism is its base. **Ask** What formula can we use to find the area of the rectangular base? [$B = l \cdot w$] What is the area of the base? [$7 \cdot 5 = 35 \text{ cm}^2$] Point out that the area is in square units.

4. Refer students to the volume formula on the board. **Ask** Now that we know the area of the base of the prism, how do we find its volume? [Multiply the area of the base by the height of the prism.] What is the volume of the prism? [$35 \cdot 2 = 70 \text{ cm}^3$] Point out that the volume is in cubic units.

5. Repeat the process with a second rectangular prism. Point out that for a rectangular prism, the formula $V = Bh$ becomes $V = l \cdot w \cdot h$, since $B = l \cdot w$. Next, work through examples of other types of prisms, such as triangular and hexagonal prisms.

Find the Volume of Prisms and Pyramids

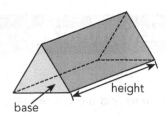

base · height

Volume of prism = Area of base · Height

$$V = Bh$$

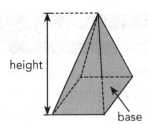

height · base

Volume of pyramid = $\frac{1}{3}$ · Area of base · Height

$$V = \frac{1}{3}Bh$$

Example 1 — **Volume of a Prism**

If the base of the prism above is 25 cm^2 and the height is 10 cm, what is its volume?

STEP 1 Write the formula.
$$V = Bh$$

STEP 2 Substitute.
$$V = 25 \cdot 10$$

STEP 3 Simplify.
$$V = 250 \text{ cm}^3$$

The volume of the prism is 250 cm^3.

Example 2 — **Volume of a Pyramid**

If the base of the pyramid above is 24 in.^{2} and the height is 5 in., what is its volume?

STEP 1 Write the formula.
$$V = \frac{1}{3}Bh$$

STEP 2 Substitute.
$$V = \frac{1}{3} \cdot 24 \cdot 5$$

STEP 3 Simplify.
$$V = 40 \text{ in.}^3$$

The volume of the pyramid is 40 in.^{3}

✔ Quick Check
Find the volume of each solid.

1 prism with $B = 23$ in.^{2}, $h = 6$ in. _____

2 pyramid with $B = 19$ cm^2, $h = 9$ cm _____

Practice on Your Own
Find the volume of each solid.

3 prism with $B = 30$ cm^2, $h = 8$ cm _____

4 pyramid with $B = 30$ ft^2, $h = 8$ ft _____

5 prism with $B = 13.5$ ft^2, $h = 6$ ft _____

6 pyramid with $B = 17$ in.^{2}, $h = 4.5$ in. _____

Find the Volume of Cylinders, Cones, and Spheres

G SKILL 23

TEACHING STRATEGY

1. **Vocabulary** Make sure students understand the terms *cylinder*, *cone*, and sphere. Items in these shapes are readily available (i.e., soup can, funnel, tennis ball), so you may want to show or have students find examples of each.

2. **Teach** Remind students that in order to find the volume of a cylinder or a cone, they must calculate the area of its base. **Ask** Looking at the volume formulas, how do the volume of a cone and a cylinder with the same height and base area compare? [The volume of a cone is one-third the volume of a cylinder with the same height and base area.] Have students look at the solids (cylinder, cone, and sphere) pictured. **Ask** What two measurements do you need to find the volume of a cylinder or cone? [radius and height] **Ask** What one measurement do you need to find the volume of a sphere? [radius]

3. **Quick Check** Look for these common errors.
   - Confusing the formulas for the volume of a cone and the volume of a cylinder.
   - Forgetting the factor of $\frac{1}{3}$ in the formula for volume of a cone.
   - Using incorrect units in answers, such as squared units.
   - Forgetting to use pi (π) or an approximation in the formulas.

4. **Next Steps** Assign the practice exercises. For students who need more support, use the alternate teaching strategy.

Additional Teaching Resource

Online Transition Guide with Reteach and Extra Practice worksheets from previous grade levels

ALTERNATE INTERVENTION STRATEGY

Materials: none

Strategy: Solve real-life problems emphasizing the difference in the volumes of a cylinder and cone with the same radius and height.

1. Remind students that if a cone and a cylinder have the same radius, then the areas of their bases are the same.

2. Tell students that a store sells frozen fruit frosties in two containers: flat-top cones and cylinders. Each pair of containers has the same radius and the same height.

3. Tell students that strawberry frosties come in 2 sizes: 96 in.³ and 32 in.³ **Ask** If the radii and heights of the containers are the same, would the container for a 96 in.³ frostie be a cone or a cylinder? [cylinder]

4. The smaller strawberry frostie described above costs $1.50. **Ask** What would be a reasonable price for the larger strawberry frostie? Explain your answer. [$4.50, since it holds three times as much and $1.50(3) = $4.50.]

5. Explain that orange frosties come in cylinder and cone containers with radii of 2 in. and heights of 5 in. **Ask** How much does a cone hold? [about 21 in.³] How much does a cylinder hold? [about 63 in.³]

6. Have students write their own volume problems for cones and cylinders, and then have other students solve their problems.

Name _____ Date _____

Find the Volume of Cylinders, Cones, and Spheres

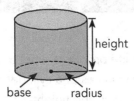

base   radius   height

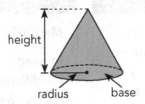

height   radius   base

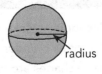

radius

Example 1

If the radius of the cylinder above is 3 cm and the height is 6 cm, what is its volume?

STEP 1 Write the formula.
$$V = \pi r^2 h$$

STEP 2 Substitute and simplify.
$$V \approx 3.14 \cdot 3^2 \cdot 6$$
$$\approx 170 \text{ cm}^3$$

The volume is about 170 cm³.

Example 2

If the radius of the cone above is 5 in. and the height is 8 in., what is its volume?

STEP 1 Write the formula.
$$V = \frac{1}{3}\pi r^2 h$$

STEP 2 Substitute and simplify.
$$V \approx \frac{1}{3} \cdot 3.14 \cdot 5^2 \cdot 8$$
$$\approx 209 \text{ in.}^3$$

The volume is about 209 in.³.

Example 3

If the radius of the sphere above is 7 ft, what is its volume?

STEP 1 Write the formula.
$$V = \frac{4}{3}\pi r^3$$

STEP 2 Substitute and simplify.
$$V \approx \frac{4}{3} \cdot 3.14 \cdot 7^3$$
$$\approx 1{,}436 \text{ ft}^3$$

The volume is about 1,436 ft³.

✔ Quick Check

Find the volume of each solid. Use 3.14 as an approximation for π. Round to the nearest whole number.

1 cylinder with $r = 4$ cm, $h = 6$ cm _____

2 cone with $r = 4$ cm, $h = 6$ cm _____

3 sphere with $r = 3$ in. _____

Practice on Your Own
Find the volume of each solid. Use 3.14 as an approximation for π. Round to the nearest whole number.

4 cylinder: $r = 7$ in., $h = 9$ in. _____

5 cone: $r = 7$ cm, $h = 12$ cm _____

6 sphere: $r = 5$ in. _____

7 cylinder: $r = 12.3$ cm, $h = 32$ cm _____

G
SKILL 24
Recognize a Symmetric Point on the Coordinate Plane

TEACHING STRATEGY	ALTERNATE INTERVENTION STRATEGY

TEACHING STRATEGY

1. **Vocabulary** Make sure students understand the terms *symmetric*, *coordinate plane*, and *reflection*. Explain that when the coordinate plane is folded along one of the axes, a point on one side will have a symmetric point on the other side. This point is called the reflection. Remind students that the equation of the x-axis is $y = 0$, since all the points on the x-axis have a y-coordinate of 0. Also the equation of the y-axis is $x = 0$, since all the points on the y-axis have an x-coordinate of 0.

2. **Teach** Direct students to Step 1 of Example 1. Review how to graph an ordered pair. Direct students to Step 2. Point out that two points that are reflections of each other in the y-axis will be located the same distance from the x-axis. Direct students to Step 3. Have them locate the reflection of point A and label it point B. **Ask** What do you notice about the y-coordinates of the points? [They are the same.] Direct students to Example 2. Tell students to imagine folding the coordinate plane so that points P and Q match up. **Ask** On what line would the imaginary fold lie? [x-axis] What is the equation of the x-axis? [$y = 0$]

3. **Quick Check** Look for these common errors.
   • Reversing the x- and y-coordinates.
   • Confusing the x-axis and y-axis.

4. **Next Steps** Assign the practice exercises. For students who need more support, use the alternate teaching strategy.

ALTERNATE INTERVENTION STRATEGY

Materials: TRT5 (Coordinate Grids), colored pencils or markers

Strategy: Draw a vertical line segment through a point to locate its reflection across the x-axis and a horizontal line segment through a point to locate its reflection across the y-axis.

1. Have students graph (5, –3) on a coordinate grid and label the point P.

2. Instruct students to draw a vertical line segment from point P to the x-axis. **Ask** How many units from the x-axis is point P? [3 units]

3. Have students continue the line segment 3 units above the x-axis and mark the point as Q. **Ask** What are the coordinates of point Q? [(5, 3)]

4. **Ask** About what line are points P and Q symmetric? [x-axis, or $y = 0$]

5. Instruct students to draw a horizontal line segment from point P to the y-axis. **Ask** How many units from the y-axis is point P? [5 units]

6. Have students continue the line segment 5 units to the left of the y-axis and mark the point as R. **Ask** What are the coordinates of point R? [(–5, –3)]

7. **Ask** About what line are points P and R symmetric? [y-axis, or $x = 0$]

8. Work through other examples with the students, asking them to locate symmetric points starting in all four quadrants.

Additional Teaching Resource
Online Transition Guide with Reteach and Extra Practice worksheets from previous grade levels

Recognize a Symmetric Point on the Coordinate Plane

Example 1

Points A and B are reflections of each other in the y-axis. If A is the point (2, –1), what are the coordinates of B?

STEP 1 Plot A on a coordinate plane.

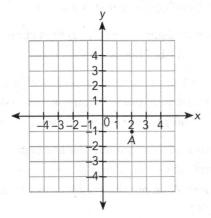

STEP 2 A is 1 unit below the x-axis, so B must be also. The y-coordinate of B is –1.

STEP 3 A is 2 units to the right of the y-axis, so B must be 2 units left of the y-axis. The x-coordinate of B is –2.

The coordinates of point B are (–2, –1).

Example 2

Points P(4, –2) and Q(4, 2) are reflections of each other in the line r. What is the equation of line r?

STEP 1 Plot P and Q on a coordinate plane.

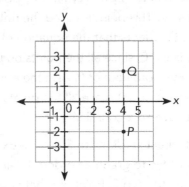

STEP 2 Locate the line of reflection. Imagine folding the coordinate plane so that P and Q touch. The crease is the line of reflection. It is the x-axis.

STEP 3 Identify the equation of the line of reflection: $y = 0$.

The equation of line r is $y = 0$.

✔ Quick Check

Solve. Show your work on a separate sheet of paper.

1 The coordinates of point R are (–4, 5). What is the distance to R from the x-axis? From the y-axis? _____

2 Points C and D are reflections of each other in the x-axis. If C is the point (3, –2), what are the coordinates of point D? _____

Practice on Your Own

Solve. Show your work on a separate sheet of paper.

3 Points P(–2, 4) and Q(2, 4) are reflections of each in one of the axes. Which axis is the line of reflection? _____

4 If a point E is the reflection of F(1, 3) in the x-axis, what is the length of $\overline{EF}$? _____

Identify Directly Proportional Quantities

TEACHING STRATEGY

1. **Vocabulary** Make sure students understand the term directly proportional. Remind them that when they graphed a direct proportion equation, the *x*-coordinate and *y*-coordinate for each ordered pair on the line were related by the same factor.

2. **Teach** Direct students to the Example. **Ask** For each pair of values in the table, what is the relationship between *y* and *x*? [*y* is always 2 times *x*.] **Ask** What does $\frac{y}{x}$ represent in the equation $y = kx$? [the value of *k*] **Ask** What equation represents the relationship shown in the table? [$y = 2x$]

3. **Quick Check** Look for these common errors.
   - Identifying *x* and *y* in an equation in the form $y = mx + b$, where *b* is not 0, as being directly proportional.
   - Simplifying one of the ratios $\frac{y}{x}$ incorrectly, resulting in an incorrect answer.

4. **Next Steps** Assign the practice exercises. For students who need more support, use the alternate teaching strategy.

Additional Teaching Resource

Online Transition Guide with Reteach and Extra Practice worksheets from previous grade levels

ALTERNATE INTERVENTION STRATEGY

Materials: TRT5 (Coordinate Grids)

Strategy: Plot ordered pairs on a coordinate grid to determine if a table of values shows directly proportional quantities.

1. Tell students that they can use a coordinate grid to determine if a table of values shows directly proportional quantities.

2. Present the following table of values:

x	1	2	3
y	2	4	6

3. Have students write ordered pairs from the table and graph the ordered pairs on a coordinate grid. **Ask** Does the line go through the origin? [Yes.] **Ask** Is it a straight line? [Yes.] **Ask** Does the line lie on either of the axes? [No.] **Ask** Does this graph represent a direct proportion? [Yes.] Tell students that since the graph represents a direct proportion, *x* and *y* are directly proportional.

4. Present the following table of values:

x	1	2	3
y	3	4	5

5. Have students write ordered pairs from the table and graph the ordered pairs on a coordinate grid. **Ask** Does the line go through the origin? [No.] Remind students that since the line does not go through the origin, it does not represent a direct proportion, so *x* and *y* are not directly proportional.

6. Provide students with other tables of values and ask students to determine if *x* and *y* are directly proportional by graphing ordered pairs.

Identify Directly Proportional Quantities

If x and y are related so that $y = kx$, they are directly proportional. k is called the constant of proportionality.

Example

State whether x and y are directly proportional.

x	3	4	5
y	6	8	10

For each pair of values, find $\frac{y}{x}$.

$$\frac{6}{3} = 2 \qquad \frac{8}{4} = 2 \qquad \frac{10}{5} = 2$$

The ratio of each pair of values is constant, so x and y are directly proportional.

✔ Quick Check
State whether x and y are directly proportional.

1 $y = -3x$ _____

2 $y = x + 1$ _____

3

x	2	3	4
y	5	6	7

4

x	4	6	8
y	2	3	4

Practice on Your Own
State whether x and y are directly proportional.

5 $y = \frac{3}{4}x$ _____

6 $y = 2 - x$ _____

7 $y = 4x - 1$ _____

8 $\frac{5}{3}x = y$ _____

9

x	2	3	4
y	10	8	6

10

x	3	6	9
y	1	2	3

11

x	4	8	12
y	-3	-6	-9

12

x	5	6	7
y	-5	-6	-7

SKILL 26 Recognize Perpendicular Bisectors

TEACHING STRATEGY

1. **Vocabulary** Make sure students understand the term *perpendicular bisector*. Remind them that two lines are perpendicular if they meet at right angles. Also remind them that, if a line segment is divided into two equal parts, it is bisected. Make sure that students recognize and understand the right-angle symbol and the pairs of tick marks that indicate congruence.

2. **Teach** Direct students to the Example. **Ask** Can a line have a perpendicular bisector? Explain. [No. A line cannot be bisected since it goes on indefinitely in both directions, but a line segment can be bisected since it has a definite length.] Which lines are perpendicular? [$\overleftrightarrow{PQ}$ and $\overleftrightarrow{RS}$] How do you know? [There is a right-angle symbol where the lines intersect.] Which line segment is bisected? [$\overline{RS}$] **Ask** How do you know? [The pair of double tick marks indicate that $\overline{RQ}$ and $\overline{QS}$ are equal in length.] Have students draw $\overline{PR}$ and $\overline{PS}$ and measure their lengths. **Ask** What do you notice about their lengths? [They are the same.]

3. **Quick Check** Look for these common errors.
   • Incorrectly identifying all intersecting lines as perpendicular lines.
   • Confusing a line with a line segment.

4. **Next Steps** Assign the practice exercises. For students who need more support, use the alternate teaching strategy.

Additional Teaching Resource
🖱 Online Transition Guide with Reteach and Extra Practice worksheets from previous grade levels

ALTERNATE INTERVENTION STRATEGY

Materials: TRT52 (Intersecting Lines and Line Segments), protractor, ruler

Strategy: Use a protractor and a ruler to determine if a line is a perpendicular bisector of a line segment.

1. Tell students that they can use a protractor and a ruler to determine if a line is a perpendicular bisector of a line segment. Distribute copies of TRT52.

2. **Ask** What is the measure of the angle formed by two lines that are perpendicular? [90°] Instruct students to use a protractor to measure the angle of each pair of intersecting lines on the TRT. Tell them to write *perpendicular* or *not perpendicular* for each pair of intersecting lines.

3. **Ask** How can you use a ruler to determine if a line bisects a line segment? [Measure the line segments. If they are the same measure, the line segment is bisected.] Instruct students to use a ruler to measure the lengths of line segments of each pair of intersecting lines on the TRT. Tell them to write *bisected* or *not bisected* for each pair of intersecting lines.

4. Instruct students to identify each pair of intersecting lines that are perpendicular and in which at least one of the line segments is bisected. Have them write the statement indicating that the line is the perpendicular bisector of the line segment.

Name _____ Date _____

Recognize Perpendicular Bisectors

Example

State whether $\overleftrightarrow{PQ}$ is a perpendicular bisector of $\overline{RS}$. Justify your answer.

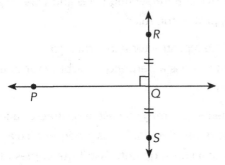

The right-angle symbol indicates that

$m\angle RQP = m\angle SQP = 90°$, so $\overleftrightarrow{PQ}$ is perpendicular to $\overline{RS}$.

The pair of tick marks indicate that $RQ = QS$, so $\overleftrightarrow{PQ}$ bisects $\overline{RS}$.

$\overleftrightarrow{PQ}$ is a perpendicular bisector of $\overline{RS}$.

 Quick Check

State whether $\overleftrightarrow{MN}$ is a perpendicular bisector of $\overline{JK}$.
Justify your answer.

1

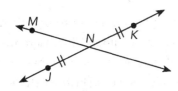

_____

2

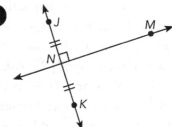

_____

Practice on Your Own

State whether $\overleftrightarrow{MN}$ is a perpendicular bisector of $\overline{JK}$.
Justify your answer.

3

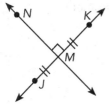

_____

4

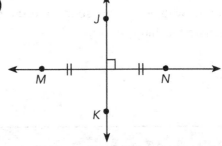

_____

Identify the Scale Factor in Diagrams

TEACHING STRATEGY

1. **Vocabulary** Make sure students understand the term *scale factor*. Explain that a scale factor is a type of constant of proportionality. Tell students that a scale model is a representation of an object that is larger or smaller than the actual object. The scale factor is the ratio of the size of its model (the drawing) to the size of the actual object. Point out that a scale factor can be a number less than 1 (for a model smaller than the actual object) or a number greater than 1 (for a model larger than the object).

2. **Teach** Direct students to the Example. Point out that the diagram is not drawn to scale, so students should use the information given in the diagram. **Ask** What is height of the window in the scale drawing? [8 inches] What is the height of the actual window? [72 inches] Make sure students notice that the same units of measurement, inches, are being compared in the ratio. **Ask** If the height of the actual window were listed in feet, what would you have to do before you could identify the scale factor? [Covert that measurement to inches.]

3. **Quick Check** Look for these common errors.
   - Mistakenly finding the reciprocal of the correct scale factor due to confusion over which value should be in the numerator.
   - Not recognizing that the scale factor can be a whole number.

4. **Next Steps** Assign the practice exercises. For students who need more support, use the alternate teaching strategy.

Additional Teaching Resource
🖰 Online Transition Guide with Reteach and Extra Practice worksheets from previous grade levels

ALTERNATE INTERVENTION STRATEGY

Materials: 3-inch, 6-inch, 9-inch, and 12-inch pieces of yarn; a yardstick or a 36-inch tape measure

Strategy: Use pieces of yarn and a yardstick to identify the scale factor.

1. Have students work in pairs. Give each pair of students a 3-inch, a 6-inch, a 9-inch, and a 12-inch piece of yarn and a yardstick.

2. Tell students to find the shortest piece of yarn. Tell students that this piece represents the length of a part of a model and that the yardstick represents the actual object. **Ask** What is the length in inches of the piece of yarn? [3 inches] **Ask** What is the length of the yardstick in inches? [36 inches]

3. Have students write the ratio of the length of the piece of yarn to the length of the yardstick. $[\frac{3}{36}$, or $\frac{1}{12}]$ Tell students that this is the scale factor.

4. Have students repeat the activity with the remaining pieces of yarn. [6-inch: $\frac{6}{36}$, or $\frac{1}{6}$; 9-inch: $\frac{9}{36}$, or $\frac{1}{4}$; 12-inch: $\frac{12}{36}$, or $\frac{1}{3}$]

Identify the Scale Factor in Diagrams

Example

An architect drew plans for a window. What is the scale factor?

STEP 1 Write a ratio comparing the height of the window on the scale drawing to the actual height of the window.

$$\frac{\text{scale height}}{\text{actual height}} = \frac{8 \text{ in.}}{72 \text{ in.}}$$

STEP 2 Simplify the ratio.

$$\frac{8 \text{ in.}}{72 \text{ in.}} = \frac{1}{9}$$

The scale factor is $\frac{1}{9}$.

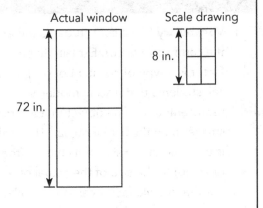

✔ Quick Check

Complete.

1

Scale Factor	Original Length	Scaled Length
?	20 ft	4 ft
3	12 cm	?
$\frac{1}{4}$	?	12 in.

Solve

2 Rashawn is making a model of a car. The car is 192 inches long. The model is 6 inches long. Find the scale factor. _____

Practice on Your Own
Complete.

3

Scale Factor	Original Length	Scaled Length
?	24 ft	6 ft
2	16 in.	?
$\frac{1}{3}$	?	15 cm

Solve

4 Patrick is making a scale drawing of a flagpole that is 360 inches tall. Patrick's drawing of the flagpole is 12 inches tall. Find the scale factor. _____

5 A rectangle is 10 inches wide and 18 inches long. Rosa enlarges it so that its length is 27 inches. Find the scale factor. _____

Solve Problems Involving Scale Drawings or Models

TEACHING STRATEGY

1. **Vocabulary** Make sure students understand the term *scale drawing*. Remind students that in a scale drawing, all the dimensions of actual objects are reduced or enlarged proportionally. The ratio between all actual lengths and the corresponding lengths in the drawing always has the same value.

2. **Teach** Direct students to Example 1. Tell students that the diagram is not drawn to scale, so they should use the information given in the diagram. Direct students to Step 1. **Ask** What does x represent in the equation? [the length of the poster] Explain to students that since the poster is larger than the painting—the original object—the scale factor will be a number greater than 1. Direct students to Example 2. **Ask** Why is scale factor squared when finding the area of the poster? [Area is expressed in square units. It is the result of multiplying one dimension by a second dimension, so the scale factor must also be squared.]

3. **Quick Check** Look for these common errors.
   - When setting up the ratio, placing the original measurement in the numerator instead of the denominator.
   - Forgetting to square the scale factor before finding an area.

4. **Next Steps** Assign the practice exercises. For students who need more support, use the alternate teaching strategy.

Additional Teaching Resource

Online Transition Guide with Reteach and Extra Practice worksheets from previous grade levels

ALTERNATE INTERVENTION STRATEGY

Materials: none

Strategy: Use cross-multiplication to solve problems involving scale drawings.

1. Draw this table and scale on the board. Tell students that the table compares the distances between towns on a map to the actual distances between them.

To go from:	Map Distance	Actual Distance
Huron to Marshall	2 in.	?
Logan to Fulton	4.5 in.	?
Anton to Beckville	?	240 mi
Weston to Trenton	?	150 mi

Scale: 1 in. = 20 mi

2. Write the following proportion on the board.

$$\frac{\text{scaled measurement}}{\text{actual measurement}} = \frac{\text{map distance}}{\text{actual distance}}$$

3. Have students substitute values into the proportion formula to identify the unknown distances. For example, to find the actual distance from Huron to Marshall, students would set up the proportion below.

$$\frac{1 \text{ in.}}{20 \text{ mi}} = \frac{2 \text{ in.}}{x \text{ mi}}$$

4. Show students how to cross-multiply to solve for x.

$$1 \cdot x = 20 \cdot 2$$
$$x = 40$$

5. Have students set up proportions and cross-multiply to identify the remaining unknown distances. [40 mi; 90 mi; 12 in.; 7.5 in.]

Solve Problems Involving Scale Drawings or Models

Example 1	**Finding length**

A painting is enlarged by a scale factor of 2 to make a poster. Find the length of the poster.

15 in.

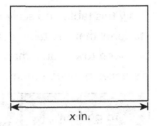
x in.

STEP 1 The scale factor is the ratio of a length in the poster to a length in the painting.

$$\frac{x}{15} = 2$$

STEP 2 Solve for x.

$$\frac{x}{15} = 2$$

$$15 \cdot \frac{x}{15} = 15 \cdot 2 \quad \text{Multiply both sides by 15.}$$

$$x = 30 \quad \text{Simplify.}$$

The length of the poster is 30 inches.

Example 2	**Finding area**

Find the area of the poster in Example 1.

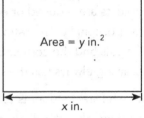
Area = 150 in.²

Area = y in.²

x in.

If two figures are related by a scale factor of 2, their areas will be related by a scale factor of 2^2.

STEP 1 The ratio of the area of the poster to the area of the painting is equal to the square of the scale factor.

$$\frac{y}{150} = 2^2$$

STEP 2 Solve for y.

$$150 \cdot \frac{y}{150} = 150 \cdot 4 \quad \text{Multiply both sides by 150.}$$

$$x = 600 \quad \text{Simplify.}$$

The area of the poster is 600 square inches.

✔ Quick Check

Solve. Use the diagram.

1 A tabletop is enlarged.

Find the scale factor. _____

2 Find the area of the enlarged tabletop. _____

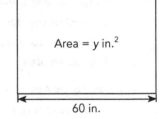
Area = 96 in.²
12 in.

Area = y in.²
60 in.

Practice on Your Own
Solve.

3 A model car is built with a scale factor of $\frac{1}{24}$. The actual length of the car is 15 feet (180 inches). Find the length of the model.

_____

4 The scale on a map is 2 centimeters : 30 kilometers. On the map, the distance between two cities is 5 centimeters. Find the actual distance between the cities.

_____

Find Measures of Interior Angles of a Triangle

TEACHING STRATEGY

1. **Vocabulary** Make sure students understand the term *interior angle*. Remind students that the sum of the measures of the interior angles of any triangle is always 180°.

2. **Teach** What is the sum of the measures of the interior angles of a right triangle? [180°] What is the sum of the measures of the interior angles of an acute triangle? [180°] What is the sum of the measures of the interior angles of an obtuse triangle? [180°] Does the kind of triangle determine the sum? [No.] Direct students to the Example. **Ask** In the equation, does it matter which angles you substitute the known angle measures for? [No.] How can you check that your answer is correct? [Add the measures of the three angles. The sum should be 180°.]

3. **Quick Check** Look for these common errors.
   • Forgetting that the sum of the measures of the three angles of a triangle is 180°.
   • Arriving at the wrong angle measure due to mathematical errors.
   • Arriving at the wrong angle measure after failing to add or subtract the same value on both sides of the equation.

4. **Next Steps** Assign the practice exercises. For students who need more support, use the alternate teaching strategy.

ALTERNATE INTERVENTION STRATEGY

Materials: TRT53 (Sum of the Angles of a Triangle), scissors

Strategy: Show that the sum of the measures of the interior angles of any triangle is 180°.

1. Distribute copies of the TRT.

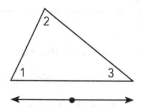

2. Instruct students to cut out the triangle.

3. Instruct students to cut off angle 1 and place its vertex on the point on the line and one of its sides along the line given on the page.

4. Instruct students to cut off angle 2 and place its vertex on the point on the line and one of its sides next to a side of angle 1.

5. Instruct students to cut off angle 3 and place its vertex on the point on the line and one of its sides next to the other side of angle 2.

6. **Ask** What kind of angle is formed by the three angles along the line? [a straight angle] What is the measure of a straight angle? [180°] Discuss that the measures of the three angles of any triangle equal 180°.

7. Have students repeat this activity with triangles of different shapes.

Additional Teaching Resource

🖱 Online Transition Guide with Reteach and Extra Practice worksheets from previous grade levels

Find Measures of Interior Angles of a Triangle

The sum of the measures of the interior angles of a triangle is 180°.

m∠A + m∠B + m∠C = 180°

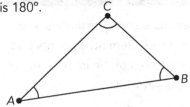

Example

The measures of two of the interior angles of a triangle are 58° and 86°.

Find the measure of the third interior angle.

STEP 1 Substitute the known angle measures into the equation.

m∠A + m∠B + m∠C = 180°

58 + 86 + m∠C = 180

STEP 2 Solve for m∠C.

58 + 86 + m∠C = 180	
144 + m∠C = 180	Add.
144 − 144 + m∠C = 180 − 144	Subtract 144 from both sides.
m∠C = 36	Simplify.

The measure of the third interior angle is 36°.

✔ Quick Check
The measures of two interior angles are given for each triangle. Find the measure of the third interior angle.

1 △ABC: 50°, 60° **2** △DEF: 23°, 106° **3** △GHI: 48°, 66°

_____   _____   _____

Practice on Your Own
The measures of two interior angles are given for each triangle. Find the measure of the third interior angle.

4 △JKL: 70°, 65° **5** △MNO: 108°, 34° **6** △PQR: 27°, 34°

_____   _____   _____

7 △STU: 91°, 18° **8** △VWX: 54°, 89° **9** △XYZ: 61°, 73°

_____   _____   _____

Find Measures of Exterior Angles of a Triangle

TEACHING STRATEGY

1. **Vocabulary** Make sure students understand the terms *interior angle* and *exterior angle*. Remind them that an exterior angle is formed by extending one side of a triangle. Review how an exterior angle is related to the interior angles.

2. **Teach** Direct students to the Example. **Ask** At which angle is the exterior angle with a measure of $x°$ located? [at angle C] Point out that angles A and B are not adjacent to angle C. **Ask** What is the sum of the measures of angles A and B? [67°] So, what is the value of x? [67] How can you check that the exterior angle measures 67°? [First use 67° to find the measure of the interior angle at C: $180° - 67° = 113°$. Then check the sum of the interior angle measures: $113° + 41° + 26° = 180°$. The sum is 180°, so the answer checks.]

3. **Quick Check** Look for these common errors.
   - Subtracting the sum of the nonadjacent angles from 180°.
   - Finding the measure of the supplement of the exterior angle instead of the measure of the exterior angle.

4. **Next Steps** Assign the practice exercises. For students who need more support, use the alternate teaching strategy.

Additional Teaching Resource

 Online Transition Guide with Reteach and Extra Practice worksheets from previous grade levels

ALTERNATE INTERVENTION STRATEGY

Materials: TRT54 (Exterior Angles of a Triangle), protractor

Strategy: Use a protractor to measure angles to show that the exterior angle of a triangle is the sum of the two nonadjacent interior angles.

1. Distribute copies of the TRT.

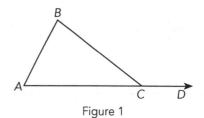
Figure 1

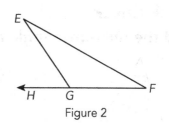
Figure 2

2. Direct students to Figure 1. **Ask** Which are the interior angles of the triangle? [∠A, ∠B, and ∠ACB] Instruct students to use a protractor to measure each interior angle of the triangle. **Ask** Which is the exterior angle of the triangle? [∠BCD] Instruct students to use a protractor to measure the exterior angle of the triangle.

3. Direct students to Figure 2. Have students measure the interior angles and the exterior angle.

4. Tell students to find the sum of the two nonadjacent interior angles for each figure. **Ask** What do you notice about the sum of the measures of the nonadjacent interior angles and the measure of the exterior angle? [They are the same.]

Name _____ Date _____

Find Measures of Exterior Angles of a Triangle

Example

Find the unknown angle measure.

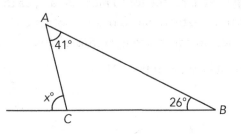

STEP 1 The unknown angle is an exterior angle of triangle at C. So, its measure must be equal to the sum of the measures of the interior angles at A and B.

$$x = m\angle A + m\angle B$$

STEP 2 Substitute the known angle measures into the equation. Solve for x.

$$x = 41 + 26$$
$$x = 67$$

The unknown angle measure is 67°.

✔ Quick Check
Find the unknown angle measure.

1
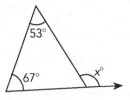

_____

2
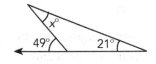

_____

Practice on Your Own
Find the unknown angle measure.

3
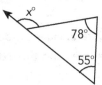

_____

4
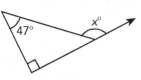

_____

5
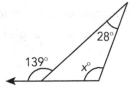

_____

6
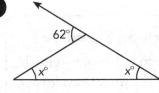

_____

Find Measures of Angles Formed by Parallel Lines and a Transversal

TEACHING STRATEGY

1. **Vocabulary** Make sure students understand the terms *parallel*, *transversal*, *alternate*, *interior*, *exterior*, *corresponding*, and *supplementary*. Explain that in this context, *alternate* means "on alternate sides of the transversal," *interior* means "inside, or between, the two parallel lines," and *exterior* means "outside the two parallel lines." Remind students that supplementary angles that are adjacent form a straight line. Using the diagrams at the bottom of the page, have students identify corresponding angles, alternate interior angles, alternate exterior angles, and supplementary angles.

2. **Teach** Direct students to the Example. Tell students that the arrows on $\overleftrightarrow{AB}$ and $\overleftrightarrow{CD}$ indicate that the two lines are parallel. Direct students to Step 1. Have students trace $\angle EFD$ and $\angle GEB$ to show that they are corresponding angles. Direct students to Step 2. Point out that the exterior sides of $\angle EFC$ and $\angle EFD$ form a straight line. **Ask** If $\angle EFC$ and $\angle EFD$ are supplementary angles, what do we know about their measures? [The sum of their measures is 180°.]

3. **Quick Check** Look for these common errors.
   • Misidentifying corresponding angles, alternate interior angles, or alternate exterior angles.
   • Forgetting that supplementary angles have a sum of 180°.

4. **Next Steps** Assign the practice exercises. For students who need more support, use the alternate teaching strategy.

Additional Teaching Resource
🖱 Online Transition Guide with Reteach and Extra Practice worksheets from previous grade levels

ALTERNATE INTERVENTION STRATEGY

Materials: wide-ruled paper, ruler, protractor, TRT3 (Blank Tables)

Strategy: Find the measures of angles formed by two parallel lines and a transversal.

1. Have students draw two parallel horizontal lines about 8 to 10 lines apart on a piece of lined paper.

2. Review the definition of transversal, a line that intersects the other two lines. Then have students draw a diagonal transversal through the two parallel lines as shown below.

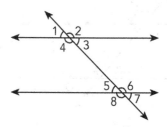

3. Distribute copies of TRT3. Have students copy the table below.

Angle	1	2	3	4	5	6	7	8
Measure								

4. Instruct students to use their protractors to measure each angle in the diagram and record their answers in the table.

5. Discuss with students the definitions of corresponding angles, alternate interior angles, and alternate exterior angles. Ask students to identify the pairs of corresponding angles and their measures, the pairs of alternate interior angles and their measures, and the pairs of alternate exterior angles and their measures. Have students make conjectures about what types of angles have equal measures. Then ask students to make a conjecture about which angles are supplementary.

Find Measures of Angles Formed by Parallel Lines and a Transversal

When parallel lines are crossed by a transversal, it produces three types of special angle pairs that are equal in measure.

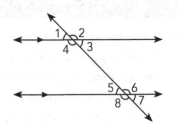

Corresponding angles: m∠1 = m∠5, m∠2 = m∠6, m∠3 = m∠7, m∠4 = m∠8

Alternate interior angles: m∠3 = m∠5, m∠4 = m∠6

Alternate exterior angles: m∠1 = m∠7, m∠2 = m∠8

Example

Find the unknown angle measure.

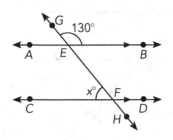

STEP 1   m∠EFD = m∠GEB, since they are corresponding angles. So, m∠EFD = 130°.

STEP 2   m∠EFC + m∠EFD = 180°.

STEP 3   Substitute the known values, and solve for x.

$$m∠EFC + m∠EFD = 180°$$
$$x + 130 = 180$$
$$x = 50$$

The measure of ∠EFC is 50°.

✔ Quick Check
Solve for each variable.

1

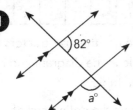

_____

2

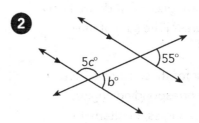

_____

Practice on Your Own
Solve for each variable.

3

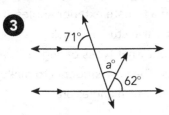

_____

4

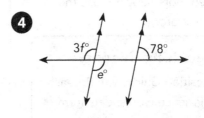

_____

Find Relative Frequencies

TEACHING STRATEGY

1. **Vocabulary** Make sure students understand the terms *outcome*, *frequency*, and *relative frequency*. Remind students that the frequency is the number of times a certain outcome occurs, and the relative frequency of an outcome is its frequency divided by the total number of all observed outcomes.

2. **Teach** Direct students to the Example. Tell students that relative frequencies are usually expressed as fractions or decimals. **Ask** How do you change a fraction to a decimal? [Divide the numerator by the denominator.] Tell students to find the sum of the relative frequencies from the table in the Example. **Ask** What is the sum of the relative frequencies? [1] **Ask** Is this true for all relative frequency tables? [Yes.]

3. **Quick Check** Look for these common errors.
   - Incorrectly identifying the total number of outcomes due to an arithmetic error.
   - When setting up the ratio for a relative frequency, mistakenly reversing the numerator and denominator, dividing total outcomes by the frequency of a specific outcome.
   - Misplacing the decimal point when rewriting fractions as decimals.

4. **Next Steps** Assign the practice exercises. For students who need more support, use the alternate teaching strategy.

Additional Teaching Resource

Online Transition Guide with Reteach and Extra Practice worksheets from previous grade levels

ALTERNATE INTERVENTION STRATEGY

Materials: 4 different colored counters or marbles, paper bags, TRT3 (Blank Tables)

Strategy: Perform an experiment and record outcomes to explore frequency and relative frequency.

1. Have students work in pairs. Prepare bags of colored counters or marbles for each pair of students. Using 4 different colors, place 20 or 25 counters or marbles in each bag. Vary how many of each color appear in each of the bags.

2. Distribute copies of TRT 3. Have students copy the table below to record their data.

Color	Number of Counters	Relative Frequency

3. Have each pair of students open their bag and count the number of each color counter in it. They should enter their data in the first two columns of the table.

4. Ask students to count the total number of counters in their bags.

5. Write the following equation on the board.
$$\text{Relative frequency} = \frac{\text{Number of one color}}{\text{Total number of objects}}$$

6. Have students write a ratio for the relative frequency of each color and enter that data in the third column of the table. Then have them rewrite each fraction as a decimal.

7. Have students put the counters back in the bag, switch bags with another pair of students, and complete the activity again.

Find Relative Frequencies

Name _____ Date _____

While waiting for the bus, Sam counted the number of cars of each color that he saw. The table at the right shows the results. Find the relative frequency for each color car.

STEP 1 Find the total number of cars Sam counted.

$$3 + 5 + 4 + 6 + 2 = 20$$

STEP 2 Write the ratio of the number of each color observed to the total number of cars observed.

Red $= \frac{3}{20}$ Black $= \frac{5}{20}$ White $= \frac{4}{20}$ Silver $= \frac{6}{20}$ Blue $= \frac{2}{20}$

STEP 3 Rewrite each ratio as a decimal. List the relative frequency of each color car in the table.

$\frac{3}{20} = 0.15$ $\frac{5}{20} = 0.25$ $\frac{4}{20} = 0.2$ $\frac{6}{20} = 0.3$ $\frac{2}{20} = 0.1$

Car Color	Number Seen	Relative Frequency
Red	3	$\frac{3}{20} = 0.15$
Black	5	$\frac{5}{20} = 0.25$
White	4	$\frac{4}{20} = 0.2$
Silver	6	$\frac{6}{20} = 0.3$
Blue	2	$\frac{2}{20} = 0.1$

✔ Quick Check
Complete the table to find relative frequencies.

1

Type of Fish	Number Bought	Relative Frequency
Goldfish	10	$\frac{10}{25} = 0.4$
Mollies	8	
Guppies	4	
Catfish	3	

2

Shirt Size	Number Sold	Relative Frequency
Small	6	
Medium	8	
Large	16	
Extra Large	10	

Practice on Your Own
Complete the table to find relative frequencies.

3

Favorite Snack	Number of Students	Relative Frequency
Popcorn	13	
Crackers	5	
Granola bars	8	
Vegetables	9	
Fruit	15	

4

Club	Number of Students	Relative Frequency
Science	24	
Yearbook	8	
Drama	20	
Environmental	16	
Service	12	

SP
SKILL 33 Find the Probability of a Simple Event

TEACHING STRATEGY	ALTERNATE INTERVENTION STRATEGY

TEACHING STRATEGY

1. **Vocabulary** Make sure students understand the terms *probability*, *event*, and *outcome*. Remind students that probability is the ratio of the number of favorable outcomes to the number of possible outcomes. Since the number of favorable outcomes is less than or equal to the number of possible outcomes, the probability of an event cannot be greater than 1.

2. **Teach** Direct students to Example 1. **Ask** What are the colors of the marbles in the bag? [green, red, and yellow] **Ask** Is it possible to choose a blue marble from the bag? [No.] Explain that the probability of choosing a blue marble is 0. **Ask** Which color marble has the greatest probability of being chosen? [yellow] **Ask** Which color marble has the least probability of being chosen? [green] Direct students to Step 3 of Example 1. **Ask** How can you express the probability as fraction, a decimal, and a percent? [$\frac{1}{4}$ = 0.25 = 25%] Direct students to Example 2. Explain that another way to ask this question is, "What is the probability of choosing a marble that is not green?"

3. **Quick Check** Look for these common errors.
   - Incorrectly finding the total number of possible outcomes, due to a computation error.
   - Incorrectly simplifying the fraction.

4. **Next Steps** Assign the practice exercises. For students who need more support, use the alternate teaching strategy.

Additional Teaching Resource

🖱 Online Transition Guide with Reteach and Extra Practice worksheets from previous grade levels

ALTERNATE INTERVENTION STRATEGY

Materials: TRT55 (Spinner), paper fastener, scissors

Strategy: Use a spinner to understand how to find the probability of a simple event.

1. Have students look at the circle on the TRT. **Ask** How many equal sized pieces is the circle divided into? [10] **Ask** What is the ratio of the pieces with the letter A to all pieces? [$\frac{3}{10}$]

   Ask What fraction of the pieces have the letter C? [$\frac{4}{10}$]

2. Have students cut out the arrow and attach it to the circle at the center to make a spinner. Explain to students that finding a fractional part or a ratio using the circle is similar to finding the probability of the arrow landing on one of the letters on the spinner.

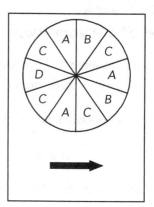

3. **Ask** What is the probability of the arrow landing on the letter B? [$\frac{2}{10}$ or $\frac{1}{5}$] **Ask** What is the probability of the arrow landing on the letter D? [$\frac{1}{10}$] **Ask** What is the probability of the arrow landing on the letter E? [0] **Ask** What is the probability of the arrow landing on a consonant? [$\frac{7}{10}$]

Find the Probability of a Simple Event

The probability of an event happening is the ratio of the number of favorable outcomes to the total number of possible outcomes.

Example 1

You randomly choose a marble from a bag holding 3 green, 4 red, and 5 yellow marbles. Find the probability you choose a green marble.

STEP 1 Find the total number of marbles in the bag: $3 + 4 + 5 = 12$.

STEP 2 Write the ratio of the number of green marbles to the total number of marbles.

$$P(E) = \frac{\text{Number of favorable outcomes}}{\text{Number of possible outcomes}} = \frac{3}{12}$$

STEP 3 Simplify the fraction: $\frac{3}{12} = \frac{1}{4}$

The probability you choose a green marble is $\frac{1}{4}$.

Example 2

Use the bag of marbles from Example 1. What is the probability of choosing a red or yellow marble?

STEP 1 Find the number of marbles in the bag that are red or yellow: $4 + 5 = 9$

STEP 2 Write the ratio of the number of red or yellow marbles to the total number of marbles.

$$P(E) = \frac{\text{Number of favorable outcomes}}{\text{Number of possible outcomes}} = \frac{9}{12}$$

STEP 3 Simplify the fraction: $\frac{9}{12} = \frac{3}{4}$

The probability is $\frac{3}{4}$.

✔ Quick Check
Solve. Show your work.

A box contains eight $1 bills, seven $5 bills, one $10 bill and four $20 bills. A bill is randomly chosen from the box.

1 What is the probability of choosing a $1 bill? _____

2 What is the probability of choosing a $1 bill or a $5 bill? _____

3 What is the probability of choosing a bill that is not a $20 bill? _____

Practice on Your Own
Solve. Show your work.

A bag holds 4 yellow balls, 8 red balls, 9 blue balls, and 3 green balls. A ball is randomly chosen from the bag.

4 What is the probability of choosing a yellow ball? _____

5 What is the probability of choosing an orange ball? _____

6 What is the probability of choosing a ball that is not green? _____

7 What is the probability of choosing a blue or red ball? _____

Identify Mutually Exclusive Events

TEACHING STRATEGY

1. **Vocabulary** Make sure students understand the terms *mutually exclusive* and *non-mutually exclusive*. Remind students that mutually exclusive events are events that cannot happen at the same time. Therefore, if two events can happen at the same time, they are called *non-mutually exclusive* events.

2. **Teach** Direct students to Example 1. Show students a fair number cube. **Ask** What are all the possible outcomes when you roll a number cube? [1, 2, 3, 4, 5, 6] What are the odd numbers? [1, 3, 5] Is 6 in this group of outcomes? [No.] Explain that since events *A* and *B* have no common outcomes, they are mutually exclusive. Direct students to Example 2. **Ask** What are all the possible letters that can be chosen? [M, A, T, H, E, I, C, S] What are the vowels in these outcomes? [A, E, I] Is the letter A among these outcomes? [Yes.] Explain that since events *X* and *Y* have a common outcome, they are non-mutually exclusive.

3. **Quick Check** Look for these common errors.
   - Incorrectly identifying all the possible outcomes of an event, resulting in an incorrect answer.
   - Confusing the terms *mutually exclusive* and *non-mutually exclusive*.

4. **Next Steps** Assign the practice exercises. For students who need more support, use the alternate teaching strategy.

Additional Teaching Resource

Online Transition Guide with Reteach and Extra Practice worksheets from previous grade levels

ALTERNATE INTERVENTION STRATEGY

Materials: none

Strategy: Identify mutually exclusive events by using Venn diagrams.

1. Draw the following diagrams on the board.

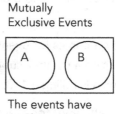
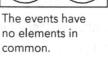

Mutually Exclusive Events

The events have no elements in common.

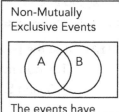

Non-Mutually Exclusive Events

The events have some elements in common.

2. Discuss how any overlap between the circles shows that two events are non-mutually exclusive.

3. For each problem, have volunteers identify all the possible outcomes for each event. Then have them draw a Venn diagram and tell whether the two events are mutually exclusive.
   - A fair number cube is rolled once.
     Event *A*: rolling an odd number
     Event *B*: rolling a 4
     [*A*: 1, 3, 5; *B*: 4; mutually exclusive]
   - A fair number cube is rolled once.
     Event *A*: rolling an even number
     Event *B*: rolling a 4
     [*A*: 2, 4, 6; *B*: 4; non-mutually exclusive]
   - Two fair number cubes are rolled.
     Event *A*: rolling a sum greater than 7
     Event *B*: rolling an even sum
     [*A*: 8, 9, 10, 11, 12; *B*: 2, 4, 6, 8, 10, 12; non-mutually exclusive]
   - Two fair number cubes are rolled.
     Event *A*: rolling an odd sum
     Event *B*: rolling doubles
     [*A*: 3, 5, 7, 9, 11; *B*: 2, 4, 6, 8, 10, 12; mutually exclusive]

Identify Mutually Exclusive Events

When two events have no outcomes in common, they are said to be mutually exclusive events. Mutually exclusive events are events that cannot occur at the same time.

Example 1

A fair number cube is rolled. *A* is the event of obtaining an odd number. *B* is the event of obtaining a 6. Tell whether events *A* and *B* are mutually exclusive events.

STEP 1 List the possible outcomes for event *A*. The odd numbers on a number cube are 1, 3, and 5. Event *A* is rolling a 1, 3, or 5.

STEP 2 List the possible outcomes for event *B*. Event *B* is rolling a 6.

STEP 3 Check for common outcomes. *A* and *B* have no common outcomes.

Since there are no common outcomes, events *A* and *B* are mutually exclusive events.

Example 2

A letter is chosen from the word MATHEMATICS. *X* is the event of choosing the letter A. *Y* is the event of choosing a vowel. Tell whether *X* and *Y* are mutually exclusive events.

STEP 1 List the possible outcomes for event *X*. Event *X* is choosing the letter A.

STEP 2 List the possible outcomes for event *Y*. Event *Y* is choosing a vowel. The vowels in MATHEMATICS are A, E, and I.

STEP 3 Check for common outcomes. Choosing A is a common outcome.

Since there is a common outcome, events *X* and *Y* are non-mutually exclusive events.

✔ Quick Check
Tell whether the *X* and *Y* are mutually exclusive events.

1 A fair number cube is rolled. *X* is the event of obtaining an even number. *Y* is the event of obtaining a 2. _____

2 A single letter is chosen at random from the word PROBABILITY. *X* is the event of choosing a vowel. *Y* is the event of choosing the letter B. _____

Practice on Your Own
Tell whether events *X* and *Y* are mutually exclusive events.

3 A fair number cube is rolled. *X* is the event of obtaining an even number. *Y* is the event of obtaining a 3. _____

4 A single letter is chosen at random from the word GEOMETRY. *X* is the event of choosing the letter E. *Y* is the event of choosing a vowel. _____

5 A number is chosen from the whole numbers from 20 to 40. *X* is the event of choosing a multiple of 3. *Y* is the event of choosing a multiple of 5. _____

6 Two fair number cubes are rolled. *X* is the event that the sum of the scores is 11. *Y* is the event that a double is rolled. _____

Answers

Skill 1

Quick Check

1. $\sqrt{45}$
2. 9
3. 0.3939..., 9, –2
4. 9, –2

Practice on Your Own

5. 13, –4, 0, $\sqrt{100}$
6. 13, –4, 2.3, $\frac{14}{5}$, 0, $\sqrt{100}$, $1\frac{5}{7}$
7. 13, 0, $\sqrt{100}$
8. $\sqrt{32}$, 0.1936...

Skill 2

Quick Check

1. 0.4
2. 0.625
3. $0.\overline{27}$
4. $1.58\overline{3}$

Practice on Your Own

5. 0.45
6. $0.8\overline{6}$
7. $0.\overline{5}$
8. 1.425
9. 1.5
10. $2.91\overline{6}$

Skill 3

Quick Check

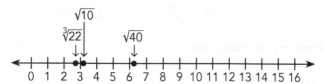

1. about 3.2
2. about 6.3
3. about –2.8

Practice on Your Own

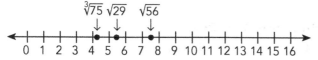

4. about 5.4
5. about 7.5
6. about 4.2

Skill 4

Quick Check

1. 7
2. –2
3. 1

Practice on Your Own

4. 3
5. –6
6. 5
7. –7
8. –3
9. 0
10. 6
11. –4
12. 5
13. 7
14. –6
15. 0

Skill 5

Quick Check

1. –4
2. 6
3. –5

Practice on Your Own

4. –7
5. 0
6. 6
7. –7
8. 3
9. –4
10. –6
11. –4
12. 0
13. 5
14. –2
15. –3

Skill 6

Quick Check

1. –14
2. 24
3. –36

Practice on Your Own

4. 10
5. –27
6. 32
7. –13
8. 28
9. –72
10. 0
11. –45
12. 36
13. 60
14. –40
15. 48

Skill 7

Quick Check

1. –3
2. 8
3. –7

Practice on Your Own

4. 2
5. –6
6. 5
7. –12
8. 9
9. –2
10. –3
11. –7
12. 1
13. 4
14. –3
15. 5

Skill 8

Quick Check

1. 82.9
2. 76
3. 1,520

Practice on Your Own

4. 128
5. 491
6. 154
7. 560
8. 6.4
9. 3,790
10. 8.6
11. 20.7
12. 95,000
13. 5,100
14. 28.6
15. 1,080

Quick Check

1. 2.9　　　　**2.** 0.063　　　　**3.** 0.521

Practice on Your Own

4. 7.28　　　**5.** 0.321　　　**6.** 4.96
7. 0.3　　　　**8.** 0.84　　　　**9.** 73.9
10. 1.6　　　**11.** 3.05　　　**12.** 0.156
13. 0.0531　**14.** 0.0986　**15.** 0.0208

Skill 10

Quick Check

1. Yes. $x + 19 = 26$ and $x = 7$ are equivalent equations. If you subtract 19 from both sides of $x + 19 = 26$, you get $x = 7$. The solutions are the same.

2. No. $4(x + 1) = 20$ and $6x = 12$ are not equivalent equations. The solution to $4(x + 1) = 20$ is $x = 4$. The solution to $6x = 12$ is $x = 2$. The solutions are not the same.

3. Yes. $0.5x + 2 = 2.5x$ and $x = 1$ are equivalent equations. The solution to $0.5x + 2 = 2.5x$ is $x = 1$. The solutions are the same.

4. No. $\frac{1}{4}x = 8$ and $2x - 15 = 17$ are not equivalent equations. The solution to $\frac{1}{4}x = 8$ is $x = 32$.

The solution to $2x - 15 = 17$ is $x = 16$. The solutions are not the same.

Practice on Your Own

5. No. $4x = 56$ and $\frac{1}{6}x = 3$ are not equivalent equations. The solution to $4x = 56$ is $x = 14$. The solution to $\frac{1}{6}x = 3$ is $x = 18$. The solutions are not the same.

6. Yes. $5x - 3 = 27$ and $4(x - 5) = 4$ are equivalent equations. The solution to $5x - 3 = 27$ is $x = 6$. The solution to $4(x - 5) = 4$ is $x = 6$. The solutions are the same.

7. No. $3.2x = 1.2x + 12$ and $x = 12$ are not equivalent equations. The solution to $3.2x = 1.2x + 12$ is $x = 6$. The solutions are not the same.

8. Yes. $2(x + 7) = 10$ and $3(x - 1) = -9$ are equivalent equations. The solution to $2(x + 7) = 10$ is $x = -2$ and the solution to $3(x - 1) = -9$ is $x = -2$. The solutions are the same.

Skill 11

Quick Check

1. $r = c + 4$; Independent variable: c; Dependent variable: r

2. $t = 5s$; Independent variable: s; Dependent variable: t

Practice on Your Own

3. $k = m + 1$; Independent variable: m; Dependent variable: k

4. $t = 9h$; Independent variable: h; Dependent variable: t

5. $P = 3w$; Independent variable: w; Dependent variable: P

Skill 12

Quick Check

1. $p = 9$　　　　　　**2.** $b = 12$
3. $a = 2$　　　　　　**4.** $y = -8$

Practice on Your Own

5. $k = -19$　　　　　**6.** $x = 9\frac{3}{5}$

7. $z = 23$　　　　　　**8.** $r = 3\frac{1}{2}$

9. $c = 2$　　　　　　**10.** $d = 3$

Skill 13

Quick Check

1. $0.\overline{3}$　　　**2.** $0.\overline{36}$　　　**3.** $1.58\overline{3}$

Practice on Your Own

4. $0.7\overline{2}$　　　**5.** $0.\overline{47}$　　　**6.** $0.3\overline{78}$
7. $0.\overline{857142}$　**8.** $0.708\overline{3}$　**9.** $1.\overline{12}$

Skill 14

Quick Check

1. Yes　　　　**2.** No　　　　**3.** No

Practice on Your Own

4. No　　　　**5.** Yes　　　　**6.** No

Quick Check

1. 0; 2; 4; 6

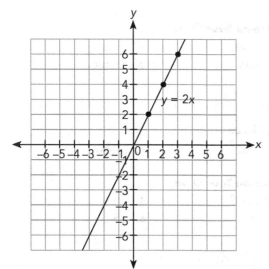

2. −2; −1; 0; 1

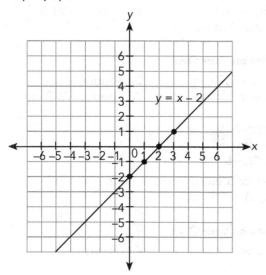

Practice on Your Own

3. 0; −3; −6; −9

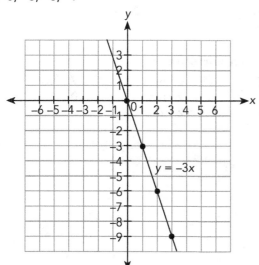

4. 1; 0; −1, −2

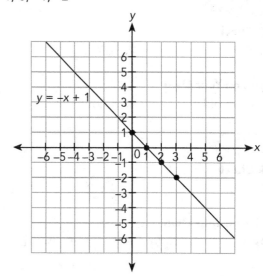

5. 6; 2; −2; −6

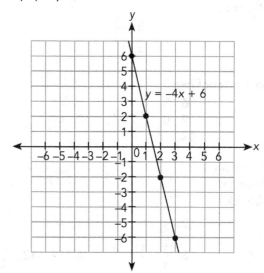

6. −5; −2; 1; 4

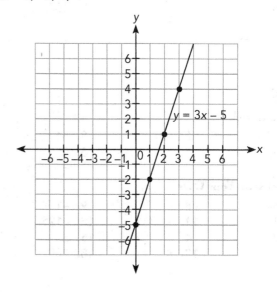

Skill 16

Quick Check

1. $19

2. $27

Practice on Your Own

3. 9 years old

4. 4 hours

Skill 17

Quick Check

1. $8b - 5$

2. $\frac{n}{5} + 3$

Practice on Your Own

3. $4x + 2$

4. $9y - 6$

5. $\frac{60}{w} - 8$

Skill 18

Quick Check

1. −1

2. $-\frac{1}{2}$

3. −22

4. 1

Practice on Your Own

5. −9

6. 5

7. −3

8. −2

9. 0

10. 4.5

11. 11

12. −3

Skill 19

Quick Check

1. −4

2. $\frac{1}{25}$

3. $\frac{1}{9}$

4. 6, −6

5. $\frac{1}{4}, -\frac{1}{4}$

6. 12, −12

Practice on Your Own

7. 64

8. $\frac{1}{64}$

9. 100

10. 20, −20

11. 3, −3

12. $\frac{1}{10}, -\frac{1}{10}$

Skill 20

Quick Check

1. 216

2. −27

3. 512

4. 2

5. 4

6. 9

Practice on Your Own

7. 64

8. 8

9. −1,000

10. 1

11. −1,331

12. −125

13. 7

14. 1

15. 3

16. 6

17. 8

18. 100

19. 8

Skill 21

Quick Check

1. 7 units

2. 13 units

Practice on Your Own

3. 11 units

4. 6 units

5. 7 units

6. 7 units

Skill 22

Quick Check

1. 138 in.^{3}

2. 57 cm^3

Practice on Your Own

3. 240 cm^3

4. 80 ft^3

5. 81 ft^3

6. 25.5 in.^{3}

Skill 23

Quick Check

1. about 301 cm^3

2. about 100 cm^3

3. about 113 in.^{3}

Practice on Your Own

4. about 1,385 in.^{3}

5. about 615 cm^3

6. about 523 in.^{3}

7. about 15,202 cm^3

Skill 24

Quick Check

1. x-axis: 5 units; y-axis: 4 units

2. (3, 2)

Practice on Your Own

3. y-axis

4. 6 units

Skill 25

Quick Check

1. Yes

2. No

3. No

4. Yes

Practice on Your Own

5. Yes

6. No

7. No

8. Yes

9. No

10. Yes

11. Yes

12. Yes

Quick Check

1. No. $\overleftrightarrow{MN}$ is not perpendicular to $\overleftrightarrow{JK}$.
2. Yes. The right-angle symbol shows that $\overleftrightarrow{MN}$ is perpendicular to $\overleftrightarrow{JK}$, and the tick marks show that $\overleftrightarrow{MN}$ bisects $\overline{JK}$.

Practice on Your Own

3. <Yes. The right-angle symbol shows that $\overleftrightarrow{MN}$ is perpendicular to $\overleftrightarrow{JK}$, and the tick marks show that $\overleftrightarrow{MN}$ bisects $\overline{JK}$.
4. No. The right-angle symbol shows that $\overleftrightarrow{MN}$ is perpendicular to $\overleftrightarrow{JK}$, but the tick marks show that $\overleftrightarrow{JK}$ bisects $\overline{MN}$. So, $\overleftrightarrow{JK}$ is the perpendicular bisector of $\overline{MN}$.

Skill 27

Quick Check

1.

Scale Factor	Original Length	Scaled Length
$\frac{1}{5}$	20 ft	4 ft
3	12 cm	36 cm
$\frac{1}{4}$	48 in.	12 in.

2. $\frac{1}{32}$

Practice on Your Own

3.

Scale Factor	Original Length	Scaled Length
$\frac{1}{4}$	24 ft	6 ft
2	16 in.	32 in.
$\frac{1}{3}$	45 cm	15 cm

4. $\frac{1}{30}$　　　5. $\frac{3}{2}$

Skill 28

Quick Check

1. 5　　　2. 2,400 in.^{2}

Practice on Your Own

3. 7.5 inches　　　4. 75 kilometers

Skill 29

Quick Check

1. 70°　　　2. 51°　　　3. 66°

Practice on Your Own

4. 45°　　　5. 38°　　　6. 119°
7. 71°　　　8. 37°　　　9. 46°

Skill 30

Quick Check

1. 120°　　　2. 28°

Practice on Your Own

3. 133°　　　4. 137°
5. 111°　　　6. 31°

Skill 31

Quick Check

1. $a = 98$　　　2. $b = 55$, $c = 25$

Practice on Your Own

3. $d = 47$　　　4. $e = 102$, $f = 34$

Skill 32

Quick Check

1.

Type of Fish	Number Bought	Relative Frequency
Goldfish	10	$\frac{10}{25} = 0.4$
Mollies	8	$\frac{8}{25} = 0.32$
Guppies	4	$\frac{4}{25} = 0.16$
Catfish	3	$\frac{3}{25} = 0.12$

2.

Shirt Size	Number Sold	Relative Frequency
Small	6	$\frac{6}{40} = 0.15$
Medium	8	$\frac{8}{40} = 0.2$
Large	16	$\frac{16}{40} = 0.4$
Extra Large	10	$\frac{10}{40} = 0.25$

Practice on Your Own

3.

Favorite Snack	Number of Students	Relative Frequency
Popcorn	13	$\frac{13}{50} = 0.26$
Crackers	5	$\frac{5}{50} = 0.1$
Granola bars	8	$\frac{8}{50} = 0.16$
Vegetables	9	$\frac{9}{50} = 0.18$
Fruit	15	$\frac{15}{50} = 0.3$

4.

Club	Number of Students	Relative Frequency
Science	24	$\frac{24}{80} = 0.3$
Yearbook	8	$\frac{8}{80} = 0.1$
Drama	20	$\frac{20}{80} = 0.25$
Environmental	16	$\frac{16}{80} = 0.2$
Service	12	$\frac{12}{80} = 0.15$

Quick Check

1. $\frac{8}{20} = \frac{2}{5}$ **2.** $\frac{15}{20} = \frac{3}{4}$ **3.** $\frac{16}{20} = \frac{4}{5}$

Practice on Your Own

4. $\frac{4}{24} = \frac{1}{6}$ **5.** 0   **6.** $\frac{21}{24} = \frac{7}{8}$

7. $\frac{17}{24}$

Quick Check

1. Non-mutually exclusive
2. Mutually exclusive

Practice on Your Own

3. Mutually exclusive
4. Non-mutually exclusive
5. Non-mutually exclusive
6. Mutually exclusive